AF176718

Gundi Gaschler:
Mr. Rosenberg and the coffee cup

Gundi Gaschler

Mr. Rosenberg and the coffee cup

Touching experiences with
Nonviolent Communication

Translated by Rudy Begas

Bibliografische Information der Deutschen Nationalbibliothek: Die Deutsche Nationalbibliothek
verzeichnet diese Publikation in der Deutschen
Nationalbibliografie; detaillierte bibliografische
Datensind im Internet über dnb.dnb.de abrufbar.

First English edition, published under license
Translation by Rudy Begas
Original title: Herr Rosenberg und die Kaffeetasse
Cover: Frank Gaschler inspired by the original
cover made by Weiss Werkstatt, München
Copyright © 2020 by Gundi Gaschler,
www.gundigaschler.com
eMail: gundigaschler@me.com

Printing and Publishing:
BoD – Books on Demand, Norderstedt
ISBN: 9783751973731

This book is also available as an E-Book

For me. Because I am worth it.

Table of contents

Preface

You should not read this book! You should hear it! From Gundi herself. I heard it. Every single touching story. **When she reads it out loud**, the world stops. A door opens and I am invited to enter. And then I see them: The Eastern European bus driver, the mother, the daughter, ..., me. And love vibrates in her voice. Love for all those people she was, when she slipped into their roles and for which she has made a place in her heart. It warms me and I feel something. I can understand every person because she understands every person. And there is space for everyone. Also, for me. And then the story ends and I see her eyes. They are shining. It is like a light, like late afternoon at the sea. Yellowish, golden, warm, **like the golden hour for photographers**. So familiar. In her eyes is water, and also in mine. It moves me, I am touched. Touched because I have seen people as they are. Sometimes complicated in what they say and do. But then quite simple, in the way they are. Quite common people, just like you and me.

If you don't have the opportunity to listen to Gundi, you may read the book. Maybe you can imagine something. Something that stands for tender-loving-care, for being held in unconditional love. For passion and for wistfulness. Open your heart and maybe you will feel this warmth, and maybe **your eyes get filled with water**.

I don't think the book is about the stories themselves. It's not about explaining or describing anything. It's more about finding the courage to see people around us with different eyes, with curiosity and welcoming everything that is. The pushing motorist, the annoyed mother, the nagging boss, the lazy children. With her eyes these are all people who have buried treasures deep inside themselves. Gundi discovers them and welcomes them.

For these eyes I love you!

Frank

Introductory remarks

About 15 years ago a friend recommended me Marshall Rosenberg's book. I already had read numerous parenting guides, and still many questions remained. I started reading it and could only stop when I finished it. For me it was like "coming home". Everything in it felt so right, felt so true for me. That's exactly what I wanted to be. At the end of the book there was a list of trainers, and I signed up for an introduction seminar with Klaus Karstädt. There I experienced magic in a role play. The tools of NVC were to be used in a conflict situation between separated parents. We started on a powder keg and ended in a togetherness that I had never experienced before. I was moved, fulfilled, my longing was awakened, my fire was lightened. That was exactly what I wanted, and I wanted it more often. I drove home and told my husband Frank that I would never apologize again (another insight from the seminar). Then we started talking as we still do today. I don't know if we would still be here today - together, if I hadn't brought NVC into our lives. I convinced him with all I had at my disposal, and he got on the boat with me. We attended numerous seminars together, and at the same time passed on what we both just learned

12

and all the things we were both so enthusiastic about in our own seminars. Again, and again I met people who were open to feel something new, to try something new in order to make a change, to grow and make their life more meaningful. I met people, who gave me their trust and let me participate in their growth, which I was allowed to accompany. Special highlights for me were always role plays. Slipping into someone else's shoes is exciting, enlightening and has taught me so much about being human. I have no idea how that works, and of course no claim that it is the truth. I only know that it is easy for me. Over the years I have grown, gained a lot of knowledge and experienced wonderful moments of encounter, also with the people who are closest to me. Some experiences touched me especially, got under my skin, changed my view of the world, were precious to me. The era of me as a trainer is now coming to an end. It is time for something new, something different. I am curious what will come. At the same time, it includes an end to my possibility of telling my stories. I would pity, that they would simply disappear. This is why I wrote them down. Probably also a little bit to make it easier for me to say goodbye. They are meant as a gift to the world. *But that sounds like a big shot now! You can't say something like that"*, I hear my inner voice saying. She does her job really well. She wants to protect me, and for that I am grateful. I had a lot of contact with her while I was writing these stories because many of them are

13

very personal. And I managed to reassure her because I firmly believe that my experiences can also move you as a reader. That is my gift. I start with experiences in seminars. The first story is intertwined with theoretical aspects for which I feel a strong impulse to share. They simply have to get out because they make such a big difference. They are followed by experiences that I encountered in "real life". Then I chat "out of the box" and reveal how things went for us at home with NVC. Finally, I go on a special journey of discovery. In the last part of this book I interviewed my daughters about how they experienced coming of age with "NVC" - parents. I asked them what nourished them and what didn't. What a brave thing to do!

As a reader I wish you many moments of "Herzspitzenberührungen". My friend Lorna Ritchie gave me this term and I love it. It is describing the moment when our hearts gently touch each other. Then it gets warm around my heart. It feels like my chest is opening up and creating space for warmth and love to be fully alive. If I let this sensation get big, joyful tears appear in my eyes. This sensation is worth being named. I will use "Heart-Touchings" to describe it.

Experiences in seminars and coaching

Playing guitar

This experience happened during a two-day introductory seminar on Nonviolent Communication for parents. On the second day we offered participants the opportunity to practice the four steps of NVC, using their own practical examples. Our main focus was on honest self-expression through role plays (scary honesty). A father wanted to try out a situation with his 7-year-old son. He asked me to play the role of his son. I very much enjoy stepping into roles because it gives me the opportunity to get a more profound understanding of everything that goes on in the boy, while I experience it myself. My trainer colleague offered the necessary support for the participant. We used laminated cards with the four steps "observation", "feeling", "need" and "request". We laid them out on the floor – one after the other, so that the participant could follow the path of the four steps. The son was sitting opposite to his father. The other participants observed the process.

The situation was: Father and son attended guitar lessons together for several weeks. The son did not want to join the last lesson, and the father wanted to know why. The father repeatedly asked his son for the reason why he was unwilling to attend. The boy did not answer, and finally ran away and locked himself in his room.

At first, we simulated the situation as it happened, in order to give me the opportunity to empathize with the son more authentically. I slipped into his role and assumed his body posture: I was sitting on the floor, my legs bent, my arms around my legs, my back bent, my head down. The father stands in front of me, bends down, speaking with a quiet and uncertain voice, "What's the matter? Why don't you want to practice now?"

In my role I hear, something is wrong with me, but I don't know what. My muscles tighten. I am insecure, confused and overwhelmed. I want to protect myself, hide away and I remain silent.

The father bends down further. His voice becomes even softer, "Is it because I play a little better than you? Should I have practiced more with you?"

Now I hear, Daddy is suffering - maybe because of me? I don't want that, but I don't know what I can do about it. I feel helpless, overwhelmed, paralyzed, and I want to run away, preferably to my room. I'm safe there. The urge overwhelms me. I jump up and run away.

My trainer college interrupts. We have enough information to try out the NVC way: Honest self-expression in four steps.

She invites the father to stand next to the first ground anchor "observation", and state which objective observable behaviour triggers something inside him.

Father, "If you sit there like that..." - he adopts the child's posture.

My college invites him to move further and step to the second ground anchor, the "feeling". She invites him to focus inside. How does it feel? What is going on in your body?

He closes his eyes and tries to feel.

She offers him different words. "Are you angry?", "Are you surprised?", "Are you sad?" – Bingo! His body reacts spontaneously. His facial expression changes and becomes softer. His body tension decreases and signals credibly sadness. His voice is deeper, powerful and stable. "If you sit there like that, I am sad…"

As a son, I immediately realize that something has changed. I get the message, Daddy is sad. Really? I didn't know that Daddy gets sad. I'm totally surprised. Sometimes I'm sad too and just knowing that Daddy gets sad too, makes me feel better. That means, that it's ok to feel sad sometimes. That means that I'm ok. I like that. Now I'm getting curious, straighten up and look at him with excitement.

My college leads him to the next ground anchor, the "need" with the hint, "... because I ...".

Father says, "If you sit there like that, I'm sad because I was so looking forward to play guitar with you".

I hear, If I don't play guitar with Daddy, he gets sad. If I want him to be happy, I have to play guitar with him. I feel tension in my throat. It's hard to breath. My muscles tighten.

My college comments, playing guitar together is just one of many strategies to fulfil a need. The question that leads us to the need is, "What is fulfilled for you, if you play guitar together?

The Father closes his eyes and investigates. Finally, he starts to smile and says joyful and with strength in his voice, "It is about companionship and being together." To me, as his son, he says, "If you sit there like that, I am sad because I like to do things together with you".

There is so much strength and clarity in his voice now. I raise my head and look at him to see if it is true, if I can trust what I just sensed. Now I heard something totally different. I heard him say that I'm important to him, and that he really wants to be with me, that he gets nourished and happy when he can be with me. I must be very special to him.

My college invites the father to the fourth ground anchor, the "request".

He says, "If you sit there like this, I am sad because I want to be with you so much, and I like to

18

do things together with you. Could you please tell me what you just heard me say?"

I answer, "Yes. I love to. You want to be with me because I am important to you. I want that too, and I already have a great idea. We could do a bike tour, just you and me?"

After this interaction, the proceedings concerning the guitar lessons and the bicycle tour went quickly, was easily and joyful. And yet there was one little thing left that I wanted to know from my father as a son,

"Are you only taking guitar lessons because of me?"

Father looks astonished to me, then his gaze wanders into the distance, his eyes begin to sparkle and shine. It's as if he's going on a journey, and then he starts talking about his dream - how we both sit at the campfire. Singing and playing guitar together on a warm summer evening. He is fully in touch with his vision and I am there with him at this sacred place.

In NVC the first step is the observation. Here we describe what triggered us in a neutral and objective manner instead of using interpretations and evaluations. The goal is that the recipient knows what I'm talking about and can agree to my reality, so that I get the opportunity to be heard further instead of landing in a yes or no discussion about the interpretations of our realities.

If the trigger is a certain attitude or tone of voice, I recommend for reasons of efficiency to demonstrate it, rather than describing it with words. As a son, the father's demonstration didn't really have an impact on me because I was not looking at him, but I didn't feel any additional resistance.

"Feelings are there to be felt," says Robert Betz in his audio book "Do you want to be normal or happy?" I fully agree with that. After the father discovered the feeling and gave it space to really feel it in his body, he seemed much more relaxed and connected to himself. That made him more present and visible to me, I really understood how he felt. Before he got in touch with his feelings, I only heard some gibberish chatter. I believe that just saying the word, wouldn't have made the change in him. It was necessary for the father to fully allow the sadness, so that he really experienced it. Only then I was able to make connection to what was alive in him. His facial expression, tone of voice, his entire appearance paired with the appropriate word and everything was congruent.

As Gundi, I was a little bit surprised that in the role of a child, I didn't feel guilty after hearing my father's

feeling. This is due to congruence. From a purely cogni-
tive point of view, I would expect feelings of guilt in this
situation. People learn fast, especially when they repeat-
edly are confronted with accusations according to the
idea "I feel bad and it's your fault!" They learn quickly
to protect themselves. In NVC, we take responsibility for
our feelings. We see them as an indicator to our needs.
We don't feel "because you..." have done something, but
"because I" have a fulfilled or unmet need. So, the core
of our feelings is based within ourselves. Another person
can merely be the trigger for them, but never the cause.

Tip: I like to use a small laminated card to illustrate this
aspect. On one side it says, "because you" on the other
"because I". If you put the page "because you" between
the ground anchor "observation" and "feeling", we are
in our old thinking pattern. If you put the page "because
I" between the ground anchors "feeling" and "need", we
enter in the NVC way of thinking and take responsibil-
ity for our own feelings.

Back to our case study, "Playing the guitar together
with you" is a strategy according to NVC definition. If
we are unable to transcend this level, we are dependent
to just this sole strategy. When my strategy succeeds,
I'm happy, if not I´m sad. That's exactly the message I
received being the son. The world offered me only two
choices: To attend guitar lessons - good, if not - bad.
Sometimes it can be a relieve, having to choose between
only two options, and to know what the consequences
are. It gives orientation and clarity. In the role of the son

21

it felt tense, without freedom of choice and therefore also without any possibility to contribute to my dad´s well-being. To be free and being in my strength is different. If we choose to take the detour through the needs and get in touch with the core of them, a lot more strategies will arise. In NVC needs are defined as abstract life-serving energies that all humans have in common. The words we use to describe them are free of involving people, actions and time. One way to find the need is to ask a question like, "What would be fulfilled when you do ... (a certain strategy)". In our example "What is fulfilled when we practice guitar together". In this case, it was particularly valuable to allow space to the father´s search, in order to find the core, which brought him to this beautiful place so close to "love".

The second way to find the needs is to use the feelings as an indicator. When we experience so called "negative" feelings, it indicates that there is an unfulfilled need, something is missing. In our example it was being together, spending precious quality time, these beautiful moments that take a very warm and special place in the father´s heart. If we now replace the phrase "I miss... (need)" or "I have no... (need)" with "I long for...(need)" or "I so much value... (need)", the focus of attention is on the fullness that is in the need. In order to dig even deeper into the power and life energy of the need, it helps to imagine a situation in which the need was fulfilled and to focus attention on feelings and body sensations that emerge. We call this "bathing in the beauty of the need". In our example the response of the father was powerful and came from the quality of touching the core energy, "Community and togetherness". As the son I even heard "love" resonating in father's expression as well, and magic happened at this moment. Dad changed so much. He was so visible, so powerful and clear, so credible. That gave me a sense of stability, security, orientation and trust. I felt carried.

The next step was the request. It is the fourth component of NVC. It contains a concretely feasible behaviour in order to fulfil the need. What exactly can the other person do now so that my need is fulfilled?

The father asked, "What did you just hear me say? Allow me to elaborate on this request form. It serves the need of understanding. I am a big fan of it. The more I pronounce it, the more I like it. I just showed myself, made myself vulnerable, shared my innermost. I would really like to know whether the essential, the core of what I want to say, is understood. If not, I try again in other words. Only when I have heard that all I wanted to say was understood in exactly the way I wanted it, is when it's useful to make the next type of requests, "How is it for you to hear that? What does it trigger in you? How do you feel now and what do you need?" This type of request opens the space for the other person's world. Only when both sides have been heard and understood, it makes sense to search for concrete, feasible solutions on the action level.

Back to the role play. Being the son, I received, "Daddy really likes to do things with me and only with me. I am really important to him. That was great. I didn't know that yet. It felt warm, sparkling and powerful. I am important to him! So important that he wants to

23

do things just with me! I immediately had a lot of ideas because I am also very smart and creative. Yes! For example, to make a bicycle tour, only me and my dad, how cool would that be? He wanted to ask mommy.

And in the end, when he talked about his dream - sitting around a campfire, singing and playing guitar together on a warm summer evening. I so much enjoyed being there with him, powerful, alive and in touch with his dreams. I have such a great dad!

And the guitar lessons were quickly resolved and the bike tour was arranged. Mom said "yes".

My personal realization being Gundi on my NVC voyage of discovery, "I can only be seen, when I show myself". In parental training I experience over and over again, parents not showing their own limits to their children, because they worry that they would limit their child too much. In my experience, this will certainly suit you for a while until the famous last straw that breaks the camel's back, then the parent explodes, and the child gets confused.

This experience was a few years ago. I wrote it down at that time, and when I contacted the "father" to ask his permission for publishing his experience, I also inquired what actually happened to the guitar lessons. They both still attend them and sometimes they play together for the rest of the family.

I want ease!

In a seminar, we were practicing the four steps of honest self-expression in subgroups. I join in as the trainer. The ground anchors are laid out on the floor. One participant stands on the feeling card and says, "I feel sad". I inquire for the observation. "If you don't want to put on your slush pants." Aha. I try to make myself useful and invite him to go to the needs card and ask, "...because you need ...?".

He says, "Well, I don't want to have a hard time".

I comment, "If we only can think of a negative formulation and we look to the opposite, we usually end up at the need. What is the opposite of "a hard time" for you?"

He thinks about it for a while, and finally comes up with an answer, "Well, I want it easy!"

Then I ask him to walk the steps again from the beginning. "If you don't want to put on the slush pants, I'm sad and I don't want to have a hard time, ..."

He takes a break and eventually says very quietly, "... I want to have it easy". He says it so quiet that his role-playing child can't hear it.

I ask, "Is it so hard for you to say that?" "Yes." "Is it, as if it is not allowed for you to have it easy?" "Yes."

I assume a whole range of core beliefs are activated. Phrases which we mostly hear in our childhood. At that time it was important that we stick to them, mostly to fulfill the need for belonging.

Many of them also served our safety or our surviving. That is why we chose to follow these phrases, why we believe them, why we internalize them and finally make them our truth. Some of them are very familiar to me, for example "Life is not a pony camp.", but also something like "The others are more important than me". Does that sound familiar to you? I myself worked on a number of them in laborious ways (because life is really hard!). I transformed a lot of them, and still new ones keep coming up. I also accompanied many people on that path and found very similar patterns. Especially with mothers, I often encountered an understanding of the role of "mother", that is characterized by (total) self-sacrifice. Mothers have no needs! Only that everyone else is doing well. And when they learn in the NVC seminar that they do have needs; it is like discovering a new world. "What? I have needs?" My answer to that is, "Yes, you do. You are a human being like everyone else. You do have needs and they are treasures, sources of strength, that serve you and keep you alive. They belong to you!"

As I'm writing this, I feel the energy rising in me. A lot of power at my disposal. I would love to shout out that message because it's so important to me. Now I ask myself, Why actually? Maybe because it was such a huge discovery for me. A real "Eye-opener". This realization stirred me up, gave me the strength to see the world through different eyes, and finally gave me a vast amount of freedom. Yes, that's what it provided. And I wish that many people may experience that.

Now I am calmed down again. So, back to our seminar situation. This is an introduction seminar. Working on core beliefs could be a precious option, but is not suitable in this case, since the topic is to learn about the four steps and get an idea of honest expression and empathic listening. Bearing that in mind, I offer the best I can think of, the best that appears feasible to me in this situation and say, "Now we practice in a role play. There is no real child and we are all here to support you. Nothing can go possibly wrong. I invite you, just to pretend, that it's perfectly natural for you, to have a need for ease. Just imagine that the most natural thing in the whole world is that you just want to have it easy for yourself, just like everyone else wants to have it easy for themselves. Are you willing to try that?"

He nods and moves to the ground anchor "observation". Now he is standing up straight. Now he speaks with a loud, clear and powerful voice, "If you don't want to put on these slush pants, I'm annoyed because I want to have ease, I want to have fun. Please put on your slush pants so we can play outside." The child responds, "Okay!"

This "Okay!" came so quick and naturally. I'm surprised and inquire. The woman in the role of the child says, "Well, it's so obvious, I want to have ease, too."

While I'm writing this story, I'm sitting in the garden. My mother squats a few meters beside me and enjoys weeding. I complain about four insect bites that have become inflamed and very hard. She immediately gets up and brings me a cooling balm. She hands it to me and says, "I can't rub it in because I'm wearing gloves, but if you're already making your hands dirty, you can also cream the sting on my arm. I was too lazy to get balm just for myself."

How fitting!

Respect – sounds familiar!

I'm a ten-year-old, growing up in the red-light district and that's where our afternoon care is closeby. My friends and I have the habit of using 'bad' word. We are now in a training practicing honest self-expression. The supervisor wants to invite me into her world. She wants to let me know how it is for her hearing these words from me and my buddies. She's standing on the observation card. In my trainer role I ask her, "What did he say?"

She answers, "Real bad words. I cannot say them out loud." Seems like they just can't get over her lips. Being in my role of the boy, I'm searching something "really bad" and offer it to her, "Wanker?" She replies, "Much worse." So, I say, "Asshole!" – even louder. We agree on this word being sufficient enough for our practice purpose.

I slide into the role of the boy and yell "Asshole" towards the hallway. The door in between is open and I sit in a position able to look outside. I say it really loud, so my buddy outside can hear me. He's out there somewhere and I hope he can hear me. Because I'm sitting here all alone like in court. I feel a little insecure although I would never admit that. I need some extra strength and a little backup. I just want to make sure he's there and reassure we belong together. This is why I'm using one of our "code words". And in my imagination, he answers.

The supervisor goes to the next card: The feeling. She searches inside herself. That's making me

29

somewhat nervous. Boys like me are never afraid. Fear is weakness and boys are strong. I already understood that! So, I shout louder, again and again and every time I am getting more powerful, stronger, safer. Finally, she comes up with something and says, "That's disgusting! I feel disgust." That surprised me fully! I expected her to scold me out or hand me a moral sermon. But instead she is disgusted? I am baffled. How is that possible? Why do our words cause disgust in her? That is so strange to me! I believe her. She really looks disgusted. But it doesn't match at all with what it means to me. I'm surprised and curious. I really want to know why, so I ask her.

She steps onto the next card and for me it gets even weirder. I feel a strong urge to use one of our "code words", but I suppress it because I don't want to disgust her even further. I like my supervisor. I like her a lot. She is one of the good ones. That's why I absolutely don't want to do anything that disgusts her. Her being disgusted is so far from my intention. It is taking her forever on that card. I really want to know why and I'm sincerely curious about what she has to say.

I skip from my child role into the trainer role and give her feedback over what is happening with the boy. I help her in finding her need, "Is it about respect?" She replies, "Yes, probably." I tell her, "Then please offer me that."

I'm going back into the child role. She says, "It's about respect." She says it so powerful. It looks like it really came from herself. Now I understand what she is talking about. I recognize respect. The first rule playing soccer is: RESPECT! So, respect is really familiar to me. It is also our highest rule among my buddies: Respect! I understand that and hey, respect is a matter of honor. I'm totally committed now. So, I tell her that it was never my intention to be disrespectful to her and that I really want to do an effort towards that goal. And yet I can´t promise that I will always succeed, but I am very willing to try so. Using our code words is more of a habit to me. I was so accustomed to it. It was so normal and also it felt so good. It is our language. When we use these words, we make clear that we belong together. Knowing that makes me strong. Unfortunately, I couldn't tell her my insides anymore because the role play was over at this point. Lunch break and afterwards we continued with other exercises.

So, what is the essence? If you want to be heard speak out about yourself. Show yourself, let yourself be seen, instead of hiding behind rules or statements like, "We don't do that here." It took the participant a lot of effort and courage to express her feelings and needs. She was rewarded by curiosity, openness and the willingness to be understood. Instead of deaf ears and letting the words pass on. In addition, it was very helpful for me being the child that she used a word for her need that I could understand because it occurs in my boy's world and that word also is of huge value to me. 'Consideration' probably wouldn't have had the same effect because that need belongs to girls. Girls are mastering consideration and are really good at it. But 'respect' - that's my job!

My insight on a meta-level: If I want to be understood by my counterpart, it is helpful to dig into his world and offer him a picture of my inner life. That's comprehendible and familiar to him and that has the same meaning for him. This is so much more effective than expecting others to immerse themselves in my world. Especially, when my counterpart is a child, having lesser experience in life.

Bruises

We attend a seminar as trainers. There is a children's home for teenagers with learning disabilities. The supervisor attempts getting into dialog with two 13-year-old boys by using a roleplay. The boys hurt each other every day. At the least there are some bruises, sometimes there is also blood and often a lot of tears. If the situation is solvable with a simple plaster, it is called a "good" day. The fact that they hurt each other causes the supervisor a lot of pain. Still she is convinced that the boys like each other.

We chose to start with self-empathy to explore what is alive in her. I invite the whole group to help her discover her feelings. This kind of method is called an 'empathy circle'. Every participant focuses on him- or herself. What is this situation or behavior triggering inside of me? How would I feel if I was the supervisor and what would I need? Then we offer our insights to the supervisor, who is receiving our empathy in form of questions, since they are just offerings. The consciousness of our own attitude, when making these offerings, is sincere curiosity, thriving on the believe that everything we do, serves to fulfill needs. We search for these valuable treasures. The intention is to support, to practice and to learn. The formulation, "Are you (… feeling) because (… need) is important to you?" Our offers may or may not be accurate for the person receiving empathy. If not, we continue to ask until we receive a convincing "yes". In my experience a visible relief occurs, when we finally reach the core, often accompanied by a huge exhale. The person receiving empathy calms down and finds inner peace. To support clarity, you can also check, "Is there more?", or, "Is that what it is about?"

In our example we discovered that the supervisor has a strong need for understanding. She really wanted to comprehend why the boys keep hurting each other, what could their motives be, since they were willing to pay this painful price on a physical level. We chose two representatives to play the roles of the boys. The three sat down, the boys side by side opposite to the supervisor. I still get fascinated how quickly people can slide into the role of playing someone else. The entire posture, movements, facial expressions and gestures of the role players have altered. The boys immediately remind me a bit of John Wayne. Sitting up straight on their chair, shoulders back, chin up, chest out, legs spread. The upper body slightly bent to the other boy. They sit just far enough apart that a little nudge is always possible.

I invite everyone to notice and focus on the body language of these boys. Their posture reveals a lot and provides me with valuable approaches, when we go searching for feelings and needs.

Now the task for the supervisor is to empathize with the boys. The rest of the group is there to support her. We guess, "You guys look very relaxed. Is that true?"

"Yes."

"Somehow you radiate a lot of strength. Do you feel strong and powerful at this moment?"

"Yes, it is like nobody can touch me. I'm in total control."

"I would like to talk to you about the injuries you inflict on each other. This is so strange to me. You guys do it over and over again and I wonder: Since you do it so often, you have to get something out of it."

"Well, you know, it's not so awful. It's all part of the game!"

"Is it like a ritual, like shaking hands, when you meet?"

"Yes, exactly."

By asking more deeply in this manner we found out that this behavior is also a good strategy to show mutual strength. And somehow this is even nurturing trust. It allows me to show my strength while trusting you to be able to handle it and that you will still stay with me. It is also about fairness and being on the same page – you're on the same level in contrast to my little brother. And on the other hand, it is all quite normal. That's life!

At this point the supervisor starts to talk about herself, how sad she feels, violence being so normal for some people. She adds that she will not give up on the boys because she really cares about them. She's convinced that there are other strategies to meet all these beautiful needs besides hurting each other. She also pronounces her deep longing to break this circle of violence that is ongoing for generations so that in the end something can change. The boys reacted astonished, "Really? Is that possible? How?"

This thinking is so different from the old mindset, "You must stop hurting each other, otherwise … (punishment or reward). It fits so much better into the world I want to live in.

In real life this would be the point where the search for new solutions could begin. Now is the time for tips and advice. The supervisor can share what strategies she has in mind, perhaps the ones she is using herself. Bearing in mind that the boys are boys and not girls. Perhaps something physical, but at least clear of violence. The boys could be inspired by her suggestions and develop their own ideas. They could give it a chance, then get back together and see if the strategies were really helpful and met all their needs. And if not, they could look for new strategies that met even more needs.

A little supplement: I'm sharing this story with my husband. When I arrive at the point where I describe the posture of the boys, he adds that many people experience such a posture as a 'provocation'. I'm surprised because I only perceived it as, "Oh man! Now we have to sit here and talk again. Doesn´t matter, I'll survive." I saw it as a resource, as a valuable strategy to deal with life. As a protective wall. And at the same time, I can well imagine that showing strength in combination with a protective wall can be received provokingly. If this is the case, the supervisor needs one or more rounds of self-empathy in which she can discover what the boys' behavior triggers inside of her in order to be open again. So, she can discover the world of the boys with curiosity.

Rules

We are at the seminar practicing empathy. We apply the empathic circle method (see previous) on real life cases. This case is about a girl - let's call her Lara. She is nine years old and in the midday care. There is this rule, 'Do not sit on tables!' The situation now is: Lara is sitting on the table, the supervisor caught her and demanded her to get off the table. Lara is responding pretty strong. She fearsome shouts at him, "You really suck, man!"

In this training situation the supervisor wants to find out why Lara reacts so harsh. He chooses to step into her role himself and shouts, "You really suck, man!" The other participants also take the standpoint from Lara's perspective by offering feelings and needs. We discovered she is really pissed off because she needs fairness and justice. It was also brought to us that the supervisor was recently sitting on the table himself, for all the children to see. Furthermore, Lara also shares her rebellion against meaningless rules. We keep on delivering new offers and get a weak "Yes, too." But a visible relief is missing. We get stuck and spin in circles on the surface. In my experience from situations like these, there is something very precious hidden at a deeper level that wants to be discovered and begs to be heard. Therefore, I inquire, "Is there more to it?" And Lara answers with a powerful voice and a load of energy, "Yes, man! I think you really suck <u>right now</u>!" The emphasis is on the words "right now". I remind myself gently not to take offence by her rejection but to follow her trail instead. So, I say, "Oh, it's only at this moment that you think I suck? And otherwise I'm ok to you?"

"Yes, man. And I don't see why you are picking on me right now! Most of the time you're actually cool."

Now I get the message: She finds me cool. She likes me. She counts on me! That causes important changes inside me. Suddenly a lot of power appears in my body. I want to choose her side! And I want to choose my side defending my values. I didn't sign up to enforce meaningless rules. No! I chose this job because I want to leave meaningful traces to adolescents. I want to accompany them growing up, be a role model, offer orientation, show them, how life works. I want to be connected to them. That is what I am here for! The rebel in me is alive and kicking: What kind of stupid rule is this? Who imposed it? A table like that can carry my weight easily and if it can carry me it certainly can carry the kids. I will sort this out in our next team meeting. I reply to her, "You know, I just realized I don't even know what this rule is supposed to accomplish. And I completely agree that it sucks and that I suck when I'm enforcing it. It's clear to me now and I will discuss it with the others when we meet next time. And if they don't come up with good reasons for this stupid rule, I will insist on discarding it. How is that for you?"

"Cool. Really cool! Thanks, man."

What's wrong with the ant?

We are doing a roleplay and I play a girl about four years old. The situation: My aunt watched me kill an ant and now she wants to talk to me about it. I am sitting on the floor looking at the ant. My aunt comes close, sits beside me and starts talking with empathy. She wants to experience the world through my eyes. Earlier on, we heard that she really likes me and that she wants to support me. She also possesses precious values and her aim is to pass them on to me. Somehow it's an educational quest that sounds like, 'Life is precious and wants to be protected and preserved'. (Positive formulations are so much more helpful than "Thou shall not kill!" because they offer direction instead of "What did I do wrong".)

She wants to connect with me and says, "Hm, the ant is not moving." That matches with my reality because I've been sitting here a while waiting for the ant to move again. I respond, "I really don't know what happened. The ant was carrying a giant something. It was so much bigger than itself. Then I thought, "It's a way too heavy for it and then I wanted to help by carrying it for the ant. So, I took the heavy load off its back and since then it is not moving anymore".

I look at my aunt with big, expecting eyes. I just don't understand the world yet and I wish so eager that my great big aunt, who knows everything, helps me out and explains me what happened, so that my world is ok again. Now my aunt glances at me with tears in her eyes and I want to know why she has tears. Most of the time tears mean that something is wrong and that is not nice. But these tears are somehow different - somehow okay. And then she says, "It is so beautiful to hear you wanted to help the ant and now my heart feels so warm, that tears welled up in my eyes".

That's such a relieve to hear. I understand that I am okay and really important to her. That I am also valuable to her and then we hug each other for a long time, and I feel held and sheltered and safe.

After a while, I realized I still don't know why the ant doesn't move anymore. So, I ask my aunt. She replies, "You know, I guess the ant broke down when you tried to help. And now it's not alive anymore." "Is it dead?", I want to know. "Yes" she says. "But that's not what I wanted at all!" There is pressure in my stomach now. This is not a good feeling. She inquires, "Are you sad?" Yes, perhaps that is the feeling. I wanted to help the ant and now it doesn't move anymore. That's not nice. "Sad" is how they call that. Yes, that could fit.

And then my aunt explains me that ants are really strong little animals. They can carry things that are much bigger than themselves. It's better just to observe them because they can quiet handle it on their own. But they can break if you want to relieve them of their load and touch them too firmly. That's nice because now I know how it works, so that ants can keep crawling on.

How was school?

It is Friday morning in my practice group. We decided to work on the topic of one of the participants. Her daughter is 14. She comes home from school. Mother asks, "How was school?" The answer is, "Ok." Then she disappears in her room. For me this topic is very familiar. That makes it so much easier for me to put myself in the mother's shoes. And when I'm in, I feel this little pain – in my heart region, sometimes less, sometimes more, depending on the content of my self-love-tank at that moment. Putting it into words it would sound like this: I am disappointed because I have a longing for togetherness, growing closer to each other and sharing a moment of juicy contact. And it just doesn't happen. It really hurts somehow. I am suppressing thoughts that say, "She doesn't care about me. I just don't matter." I am also eager to be a part of her life. Perhaps I'm even a little sad and lonely. These two feelings thrive on a deeper layer and while I am writing this down, I notice that I rarely allow myself to feel them in day to day life. Maybe because I'm under the impression I can deal more easily with the other feelings. That sucks! But that's another chapter.

Back to our practice group. We start with empathy for the mother. I offer her my findings. She recognizes herself in it and wants to be involved in the world of her daughter. I offer myself for playing the role and she agrees. So, I am 14. I come home from school and encounter my mother. She asks, "How was school?" I answer, "Ok."- and turn away slightly. My focus goes inward, I allow the remains of the day to pass before my eyes:

It was quite normal. As always. Many pupils, a lot of noise - especially the minors are so loud. During the lessons: Sitting, trying not to stand out in a negative way, don't annoy the teacher, but showing up, just enough to be noticed. That is important for the oral grades. Pretending to be interested. Keeping all emotional impulses, like frustration or anger in place. Not showing I was really bored. Wrapping up all my gear at the end of each lesson. Rushing to the next classroom. Queuing up for a butter pretzel at the kiosk for ages. Two teachers were testing us. This always makes me anxious, rather they pick me or not? Today was my lucky day. Some others got the full load - and they managed it pretty well. In math class I didn't grasp a single thing, as always. This teacher is incapable of explaining anything. At least not in a way I'll understand. That's annoying, but it's business as usual. In Religion class I played poker. Some of my girlfriends thought we were getting a test today. I didn't think so and, in the end, I was right. Thank God! I barely glanced at my notes in the previous break. The English teacher made a pun and only a few others and me got it. We laughed our asses of. I like English, I am really good at it, too. Then I tried to organize my birthday party with my friends. I inquired what they like, but didn't get a clear answer. That's really annoying. On my way home, I was lucky, I managed to get a seat on the bus. That was it so far, my day. Nothing extraordinary. Nothing worth mentioning. Just "OK". Now, I am glad that I am home. I just want to leave all this behind, chill, relax and finally have some peace. Later on, I'll be doing my homework and practice the piano and somewhere in between I also want to live a little and do stuff for myself. Something beautiful that I really enjoy. I look up at my mother. Oh dear, she looks tense. When she looks like that, she usually wants something from me. Then we have to talk for ages and she tries out this NVC stuff on me again and talks about feelings and needs and then I also have to take care of it. That doesn't suit me at all.

I step out of the role of the girl, get up and go standing next to the chair I just sat on as a daughter. I share what I just experienced. We agree that a conversation at this point doesn't make any sense. Instead we delay it until the dust settles. I sit down on the chair again and slide back into the role of the daughter. Mother says, "When you come home from school, do you just want me off your back and leave everything behind you?"

"Yes."

"And, when you hear me asking how school was, does it annoy you?"

"It's annoying when you keep poking. If I say it was OK, it was OK! I just want you to believe me. That's all you need to know. I'll manage perfectly on my own. I am no longer a baby. I no longer want you to interfere and go to the teacher. I am perfectly capable of handling it myself, you know?"

"I hear you want to take care of your school affairs yourself and that you want me to stay out of it."

"Yes, that's right. It's more than enough that I get annoyed. It's really not helping if you get upset, too. By doing so, you make things even worse. And when you go to the teacher that is so embarrassing. That's like admitting I need help from my mother because I can't handle it on my own. Do you think, you can do that for me?"

I slip out of the role again asking the mother how that landed for her. We discovered she is now ready to redefine the relationship with her daughter. It will take a lot of trust and that she wants to try to let go. And that's literally what she says to her daughter, "Yes, I think I can do it. It makes sense to allow you your own experiences of which you can be proud of. And that my job now is to trust you. I'm willing to try it, but I can't promise that I'll always comply. And when I catch myself, as my maternal protective instinct is taking over, I want to check carefully whether I have enough trust. And if not so, I want to let you know, so we can find out together what needs to be done or not. And I want you to know that I am always here for you whatever happens. I'm here to support you in any way. How does that sound to you?"

"Good. I am relieved. Together we can manage. You stick to your part and I stick to mine. And if one of us needs support, we'll have it. That sounds so much better than: Mama will fix it for me."

"Yes, it's more on an eye-to-eye-level, as if I fix everything for you."

After a little pause mother adds, "There's one more thing I want to tell you. I'm still interested in you and I still want to be involved in your daily life. I love to know what's on your mind, what you're experiencing, even the little things. Things that may not be so special or worth mentioning. Are you willing to share them?"

I'm surprised. "But Mom, you don't tell me anything about you either!"

"That's right! You're absolutely right. I just realized I don't do that either and I wonder why. Probably because not so much happens in my life – only little things. Do you want to hear them?"

"Whenever I have time, I want to. For instance, now would suit me." And the mother begins to talk about the little things she experienced that morning, how she did her colleague a little favor, all the thoughts she had about what she was going to cook later on and what it was like, when she was shopping for the ingredients and that things got hectic after all because of the phone call with her friend... and in some sort of magical way, out of nothing space appeared. Space for the little things. Nothing special or particularly exciting, but beautiful anyhow. All these little treasures that she experienced. And when the mother was finished and paused for a brief moment her daughter took over and began to tell her story. Little treasures ... and everybody in the room was bathing in an ocean of astonishment of how valuable little things can be, whenever they get space.

When my daughters came home from school that day, we sat on the terrace for dinner. I shared what I experienced in the practice group that day and mentioned the magic space that appeared between us. The plates had been finished for long and still we hadn't finished telling stories about our little things, when my mother came up the stairs from the garden for a brief request. She resides on the ground floor of the same house. I invited her to join us. Usually she doesn't stay because she doesn't want to be a burden and then she leaves right away. At the most she sits on the edge of the chair, ready to jump up instantly to disappear any given opportunity. On that day however she sat down with us on the whole surface of the chair and she even leaned back. Everyone was astonished. Then she started to talk about her little precious things ...

Since this moment I have been into this theme topic of space: taking space, giving space, creating space, occupying space, freeing space, allowing space, granting space. Very exciting!

You are liars

We are in a 9-day intensive seminar. In a group of three, we are sitting in a meadow on a blanket, underneath an apple tree brimful of ripe apples. A magical place full of strength with a nice view in the distance.

A participant cares to work on her topic and we support her. She entrusts us with things she did as a teenager. Things she is still ashamed of. So ashamed, she repressed them, packed away this part of her life. She lost herself in men, drugs and alcohol more than she wished to admit now. In the present and being at this powerful location, she is ready to face this part of her life, hoping to find some peace about what she experienced back then. We agree on doing a role play. She chooses to observe. I slide into the role being her at the age of 20. The third person in our group will try to understand my world. So now I am 20. I turn away. I am pissed off and I feel disgust. I hear her asking, "Would you be willing to tell me how you are doing right now?"

"Not a chance!"

Pause. She makes further attempts, which pass me by. I perceive it like some futile background noise. And still she remains persistent. She keeps probing me with her questions, over and over again. Something is happening inside of me. This is new. Somehow it occurs funny, since nobody is interested in me. I snap at her, "Nobody cares how

I feel anyhow!" and turn away from her. Still she persists in asking me. Now I'm getting confused and, in a way, it makes me curious. I clearly stated my business, and yet she keeps probing. I feel tense, even a little skeptical. Is she really interested? A spark of hope appears. It would be nice, if somebody was interested in me and at the same time, I doubt it so much.

All of a sudden, the participant, who brought her topic in, gets up and enters the roleplay. Previous she was lying next to me, observing. Now she looks straight into my eyes. That is totally different, more credible. I'm astonished. Keeping the eye contact, she speaks, "I want to know. I'm interested in you." I grow soft, still very skeptical, but softer. Soft enough to say, "Everything is a damn lie anyhow".

"What do you mean by 'damn lie'?"

I shout, "You all pretend your world is so great and then you expect me to behave likewise. I can't do that. I don't believe your world is so great!! There are so many things wrong which I don't like at all. And still you insist to pretend everything is all right, while I clearly see that is a damn lie. You are liars! You lie to yourself. I never want to become someone like that!"

"So, this is about honesty?"

"Hell, yes! If at least one of you had the courage to say, 'Yes, life sucks. I am unhappy', or even, 'I am sad' or 'I just don't know it anymore'. THAT would be honest! Instead you pretend that's just the world you have to live with. That I just have to

49

adapt it and go along. But I don't want to adapt to something like that. Get the point?"

She replies with a loud voice, "I hear you want an honest answer, the truth about how we are really feeling. Is that correct?" I yell back at her, "YES, looks like you finally got it!!"

She speaks with loud voice which I so much enjoy because we're in the same power now. I say, "By the way, I am happy you're still here. That you did not flee like everybody else does, when I start screaming and slamming the doors!"

She replies, "Is it so relieving for you being able to say everything, in the intensity of what it's like right now and that someone present is able to bare it?"

"Yes, I'm so f***ing angry. This is why I shout. That's me being honest. You got me?"

"Yes, I see that you're angry and damn brave enough to admit it, show it and yell it since it's you being honest and defending what's important to you."

I calm down a little bit. "Exactly. And it's good you don't flee nor that you are afraid of me. That's really good because otherwise I tend to think there's something wrong with me that I'm a weirdo, you know?"

"I imagine that must feel quite lonely?"

"Yes, and quite wrong, too!"

"And now it feels good to realize that someone can bare it?"

"YES!"

50

At this point the participant who introduced the topic, steps out of the roleplay and says, "I want you to know I understand it now".

"What do you understand?"

"I understand that you were lonely and angry. I was indeed angry and very lonely at that time. My mother endured everything and that was absolutely not ok for me. It made me so angry and that gave me even more rebellion power. That power is still present. Meanwhile I managed to deal with it. But back then, I felt lonely, all alone. I felt like an alien because I didn't know anyone who felt the way I did. It's really sad not knowing for so long I was lonely. I did stupid things to get out because that was the smartest thing that came to my mind at that time. Thank you for making that clear to me. Now I understand it was ok to be like that. Not "good", not "bad", just ok. That feels more peaceful now. This is my first step to face this subject. It will certainly need more steps. For now, it's enough.

On the way back to the seminar I talked about an encounter with my daughter. Sometime in her puberty she came to me and asked, "Mama, are you happy?" I immediately reflected, "Am I happy? Do I do enough to be happy? What do I exemplify? Do I take enough care of myself?" Then, it occurred to me, that maybe she is talking about herself and I ask, "What do you mean by that?" She says, "Well, i you're happy, I'll do it your

51

way." I felt like a relief. And then we had a long talk. I told her about the decisions that I made in my life, which I am satisfied with today and also about the ones that I would make differently from today's point of view.

Are you suffering?

We are once more in a multiple day seminar. A participant requests an individual session. Her topic: Her partner is experiencing depressive phases. Whenever that occurs, he withdraws and doesn't want to see anyone not even her. She suffers and feels helpless. She loves to support him but fails to see how. She tried to raise the issue, but he dodged the matter. Now she seeks answers for her questions and asks me to slide into his role. I`m willing and able to tell her my truth.

I start, "What do you want to know from me?"

She says, "How do you feel, when you - well, you know...?"

"Do you have a hard time to pronounce 'it'?"

"Yes, it's like a 'We Don't Use That Word', a taboo. Something nobody speaks out loud. And there is also something else: I think, by pronouncing it out loud it is like creating its reality, it is becoming real. Then it's the truth. If it remains unspoken it is less threatening and perhaps also easier to repress again. Interesting, I wasn't aware of that yet."

"Would you like to do a little more research on this aspect?", I ask.

She wants to stay in the roleplay and replies, "No, I'd rather know how it is for you to be present in one of your phases."

I take some time to look inside and answer, "Actually it's quite good here. It is quiet inside, well known, familiar, somehow it feels even safe."
She looks surprised, "Quite good?! But aren't you in agony?"

"No. It's more like that there is nothing at all. No suffering, no pain, no sadness, no fear, no danger, no worries, no ailing either. Everything is just being. Being neither good nor bad. Just being. That's all there is to it. No feelings. Just quietness, indifference, nothing else."

"In that case there is no joy either? That must be painful?"

"That's correct, the joy is absent, but it doesn't matter. It's ok, not good and not bad either. It just doesn't matter."

"But it must be horrible not to feel any joy."

"Is it horrible to you?"

"Yes, it is already hard even to imagine it. Isn't it very lonely to be all alone and feel nothing?"

"Yes, it is somehow lonely. There is only me, my core and around it is a huge solid wall keeping everything away from me. It protects me so nothing can harm me. But it's not bad at all, it's ok. What do you hear me saying?"

She needs some time to reflect on her answers, "I hear, that you are not in pain. That it's somehow ok for you. Even safe"

"Yes, exactly. And how is it for you to hear that?"

"Phew, new. Yes, very new, I guess. I really thought you were suffering and that was difficult for me. But hearing that you are pretty ok makes it more bearable for me. I am actually relieved now. Is there more you can tell me?"

"Yes. If I am in that phase the only thing I have to look after is myself. And I can cope with that. I'm confident that someday this phase will be over and that I will survive. All I have to do is wait out the storm. I can manage that as long as I am only responsible for myself. What do you hear now?"

"I hear that you are quite confident to overcome this phase and that you just have to wait it out which you can handle."

"Yes, that's it. And how is that for you?"

"Less threatening yes, much better. I'm hearing you are pretty confident to overcome this in your own way. You really believe this approach of you will work, so I start believing it, too. Wow! My perception definitely changed now. Before, I had a hard time feeling powerless, helpless, unknowing what to do to help you while you were in agony. But now, knowing you don't suffer, you don't need any help. I'm still astonished about this insight. It will take a while until I really grasp it. I probably have to remind myself over and over again until I truly believe it. It might sound like, "He's doing the best he can at the moment and that's ok." Or shorter, "It's ok". Or, "It is what it is."

Her entire energy had changed distinguished, you can tell by her shining eyes. It is like the huge dark clouds that were hanging above us dissolved completely making space for confidence and vigor energy. "I'm so excited now. Instead of being help-less, I found out there is actually something I can do. Perhaps there are even more possibilities to make it easier for you?"

In my role these words go deep. Sadness appears and tears are flowing. "I hear that you really care to support me. It sounds like music to my ears and at the same time it is tremendously hard accepting your support. While I'm depressed, I see myself as a burden for the people close to me. It torments me when I'm unable to be there for them. It is out of balance, unfair. It is so hard for me to accept your support since I will never be able to give it back likewise. I really would like to be an equivalent partner to you and at the same time I can't guaran-tee not getting depressed again."

She says, "I hear you are longing for fairness and balance between what we put into the relationship and what we get in return?"

"Yes, exactly."

"Okay. I want to assure you that I really gain a lot from our relationship. Being together with you nourishes me on so many levels that I do experi-ence my giving and receiving in balance. For better or for worse. I am here and I pose you all these questions because you are worthy, because we are worthy to be, because I believe in us and I want to know how we can manage it properly. I care to support you. Do you believe me?"

More tears are flowing now, it is so hard for me to believe that. Believing that I - as I am – in the state I am - can be so valuable to someone. I say, "If you say it like that, I'll do my utmost, even if it's hard for me."

"Okay. Can you tell me what could make it easier for you when you are depressed? I want to stand by your side and go through this together with you. What would help you?"

I answer, "When I am back in this 'normal' world I feel like a failure. I am ashamed of being weak over and over and again. And the worst thing for me is knowing that the people close to me are suffering from my condition. It would help, if I knew that you would outlive my depression unharmed. If only I knew, you were not in pain… You do suffer, don't you?"

"Well, I did suffer until now because I thought you were in pain. But from now on it can be different. By learning to trust you are somehow ok, I won't suffer anymore. I am willing and able to do that."

"Ok. What else made it hard for you?"

"Your eyes, they are so empty, lifeless. I can look right through you. There is no resonance. It is like only your body is present and your soul is drifted away. That what makes you a human is simply no longer there. That scared me, I lost contact and I didn't know how to reach to you."

"You long for contact?"

"Yes, if only I could be with you and knowing that it is ok to be with you that would be nice. Until now you always sent me away. I took it you won't want me around. Did I get that right?"

"Yes. I sent you away because I didn't want to pull you down with me. Do you think you can be with me without being pulled down by me?"

"I can give it a try. I could visit you whenever I'm emotionally strong enough and I could leave you, whenever I'm depleted and then I will do something nice to regain my strength. Would that help?"

"Yes, very much. And perhaps, if you are with me, you could hold my hand. That would do me good, I think. Just being by my side without any expectations and holding my hand. I could accept your presence and maybe even enjoy it. You could visit me in my world and just be with me, without the urge to bring me back into your world. Would you be willing to do that for me?"

"I like that image. You are in your world and I am in mine. I pay you a visit in your world and then I go back to my world. With this image in mind, it might work out fine. I definitely want to try it. Did I also understood that you decide when to come back into this world?"

"It doesn't really feel like my choice. It's not something for me to decide. The only thing I know, is that dragging doesn't work."

"Ok, I got that. I just need to be patient. There is one more thing a burning question: Can I really count on it that you will come back one day? Are *you* sure you will come back? Do you really know that? Can you trust yourself about that?"

"What do you mean?"

"Can you promise me that you won't kill yourself?"

"Oh, promise... phew, I don't think I can promise that. I've thought about it several times now, but not more than that, just thought about it. And right now, I really want to be honest with you. I would be lying if I said I could promise it."

"Can you perhaps promise me to tell me whenever you start thinking about it again, so that we can get help?"

"Yes, I could write it on a scrap of paper. That is definitely possible, writing is possible, I know that for sure. I can promise you that."

"Wow. Thank you."

We sit side by side in silence for a while. Then she starts to speak, "Earlier I heard you say you feel like a failure and feel weak because you are going through depressive phases?"

"Yes."

"A new image just came to me. I realized that for you this depression can be a place of rest, to recover, a place of retreat, a protected space, that provides safety. That makes your depression a valuable strategy. Similar to a cold. My body switches down and forces me to rest, or gives me a clear sign, that it is time to slow down. Does that make sense to you?"

"Yes, it does. But this strategy comes with a price and maybe it makes sense to look for other possible approaches in real life."

"Yes, it does." she says. She steps out of the role play and is speaking to me being Gundi again, "I will tell my partner about our role play. I'm ready to go through this together with him and I firmly believe that we can find ways to support each other in this."

Doomed to watch

Another nine-day seminar. A participant - let's call him Robert – asked me to do an individual session with him and his new partner. They are recently in love and they look so happy together. His topic: He yearns for connection with his 30 years old son. Contact is scarce. And every time they meet it's exhausting, like a dance on very thin ice. Each word carries the potential to be misunderstood while he craves real contact. I asked when this started. He replied, "Our relationship is like this, since my wife, his mother, died of cancer a few years ago. In the end we were all present, supporting her and each other. Everyone, except my son. He has remained absent for the final three weeks."

I wondered what that evoked in the father. Maybe some resentment or disappointment? He says, "No, it was more like: We are not fully present, there is someone missing. I have a hard time finding the right word for this feeling. 'Incomplete' comes closest. There's no grudge, no accusation, I just want to comprehend it."

I offer him to slide into the role of his son. He agrees but first wants to share one more important notice: How much he really appreciates his son. Even stronger than that, he admires him. When his son was 17 years old, a friend of the father who was a surgeon, took his son to a surgery. When his son came home afterwards, he said, "I know what I want to become: A surgeon". From that moment on, he went straight to this target. And he succeeded. Today he is a surgeon. "I am so proud of him", the father ends.

Now he is ready to meet me in the role of his son. I slide into the role and say, "Ok, father. What do you want to know from me? I am here to tell you my whole truth."

"Why weren't you present, when your mother died?"

"I could not bear it. It hurt me so damn bad. I couldn't stand it no longer to watch her diminish and fade away. The worst of it all was me, unable to help her. Me, having this degree in medicine to perform miracles and make people healthy. I was reduced to be just a bystander, unable do anything more than observing how nobody, absolutely nobody, could help my mother. That was so unfair. I was so furious at the world. My worldview was shattered. That's the reason I stayed away. Because it hurt so much".

Father cries for a long time. I am with him. It's okay that he cries. Finally, he says, "Now I understand. It was awful for all of us, and best way you saw to deal with it, was to stay away."

"Yes. I know that all of you were present until the end. I also know that you really wanted me there, but I just couldn't do it."

"It's okay. I understand it now." More tears flowing abundant from both eyes. And they are welcome in this precious, sacred space. There is so much room here for all the tears to be let out. Then father says, "You know, I'd like to have more contact with you".

And as a son I respond, "But you are so different from me. So sensitive and understanding. You are worlds apart from my concept of life. For me, it's all about being clear, I know what I want, and then I go for it head on, like a man. I love the thrill of the risk and I fancy a beer now and then. Talking and understanding each other is not my way. That doesn't serve me at all."

At that moment the magic happens – a major turnaround, the full 180 degrees. The father adjusts his posture. He straightens his back and is now sitting upright, showing his full size. Also, his tone of voice changed now, he sounds utterly determined and crystal clear. He appears completely confident while saying, "Hey, let's have a beer together, shall we?"

"Absolutely."

My learnings as Gundi: If you want to have contact, meet the other in his world instead of expecting the other to meet you in your world.

Are you really interested in me?

Another seminar lasting for several days. I am attending as a participant. We paired up to practice the four steps of honesty. I am with a young woman, age 25. From my opinion, she looks beautiful. She has long blond, curly hair that looks so playful. I have to restrain myself not to grab one of her curls. I gently want to pull and release one of them, just to see if and how it twirls back into position. How often will it spring up and down until it comes to a rest? She has a slender figure, about 1.75m tall, has an upright posture and looks very self-confident. She has soft facial features and expressive eyes. I´m both curious and excited about meeting her. We were granted 30 minutes to practice. The place is crowded, and we agree on practicing outside. It is past sunset and getting a little chilly. We walk side by side and she starts speaking about her father. "He is not really interested in me. He wants to know how I am, and when I start to talk, he interrupts me by talking about himself, about other people or about politics".

"This is funny", I say. "We have got that in common. I also have a person among my relatives, who acts exactly the same. Looks like we've got similar issues." We are amused, amazed, relieved and delighted that the universe - or whatever - brought us together. We start to search for our feelings, when we experience such a situation. There is definitely some frustration, since we like to be heard. Also, disappointment, because we have the idea that the other person shows no interest. Underneath this, we discover a longing to be important and to matter to the other person.

And then, of course, there is also indignation, "Hello-ow? First, he asks me how I am. And then he doesn't care to know!" There is a longing underneath this, for honesty and to be taken seriously.

Another voice says, "Hello, don´t fool me!" Underlaying we uncover that we want to be sure the question is seriously that we can trust the words of the other. Having plenty of empathy for ourselves we decide at this point to at least have a peek from the perspective of our counterpart. We choose a role play.

I slide into the role of her father and change happens instantly. I have more body tension now and I stand straight. My daughter is facing me, and I feel a bit restless and agitated. Something is wrong and I am vigilant, about a 6 on a scale from 1 to 10. My senses are sharp. I am on my guard. She starts to speak, "There is something I want to discuss. It burdens me and I would like to understand it and, if possible, change it, so that it's no longer a burden to me. Would you be willing to look on it together?"

My fatherly instinct is alarmed. My little girl feels troubled! I definitely want to contribute bringing her world back in balance. That's my sacred duty as her father. Even if I have something to do with it myself. It may be uncomfortable, but I will take it like a man. After all, I even would fight dragons if they threatened my daughter. So, I say, "Yes, of course."

She continues, "Earlier on, you asked me how my seminar was. After two of my sentences you started speaking. Did you notice that, too?"

"Yes, really? After the second sentence? I remember something occurred to me and I wanted to tell you right away. Was that wrong?"

"Well, what came to me, was that you weren't interested in me. Is that true?"

"No!" I answer. I am horrified. "Of course, I'm interested in you! Otherwise I wouldn't have asked how it was!"

"And that's exactly what confuses me. You ask me, and then you don't want to hear me out at all. So, how about it?"

Damn, she's got a point there, I hadn't looked at it like this. I choose to be honest and tell her my whole truth, even if that gets me way out of my comfort zone. I am a little embarrassed, but I want to come clear on this one. "Okay, when I'm asking you, I just want to hear that you are happy that you have a grip on your life that everything is in order. Perhaps also that you encounter beautiful things and that you are glad. Being happy is perhaps a bit too much to ask, I would settle for content. In that case, I know I don't have to worry. Then I am reassured and at ease, so I can mind my own business in peace. Because there is no pressing task for me to attend. But if there is something that burdens my sweet daughter or is troubling her, then I want to be the first to know. Absolutely. In that case, I will take a stand and fight the evil dragon!"

She stops and looks at me. Her eyes look soft. "It moves me, that you want to support me whenever I need you. I'm aware of that. It feels damn good knowing that. My big, strong daddy, who always stands by my side, no matter what stupidity I just pulled off. You always stood behind me and supported me. That is very assuring. This knowledge provided me with strength and courage, and I am grateful for it."

As a father I'm relieved. Hearing that really feels good. Yes, that's what I always wanted her to know, and it's good to hear that message arrived. It provides calm, I feel relaxed and comfortable now. We look each other in the eye - there is so much warmth. We hug each other for a really long time.

After a while something starts to tingle in me. "You know, when you go to these self-discovery courses, it's a little frightening to me. That is so far from my world. I imagine it to be so esoteric crowded by people who have no grip on their lives. And you being in the middle of them. Do you have a handle on your life?"

"Would you like to be able to trust that I have my life under control?", she asks.

"Yes.", I answer.

She continues, "In my perception, I believe I do. I'm working to achieve it, that's exactly why I'm attending such seminars. I want to shape my life in the best possible way. I want to make conscious decisions instead of being the puppet-on-a-string in my own life. That's exactly what I learn there: to take responsibility for the things I can influence and to let go of the ones I can't. I get to know myself, discover why I act in some situations like I do. And if I don't like it, I learn to react different. How does that sound to you? Still frightening?"

I answer, "Hm, no. It sounds rather reasonable. And not esoteric at all!"

She goes on, "Not according to my understanding. We don't worship giraffes and we don't read our future from glass balls or something. At the same time, even for me there are some things difficult to understand. For example, when we are in role-plays. Often, I experience that the person taking on a certain role, speaks exactly the same words actually said by the person who he represents. And that's hard for me to understand. I have a hard time believing that or explaining to myself how it works. But then again, I experienced it so often now that I can't do anything else then to believe it is true. Is that frightening you?"

I say, "No. After all, you still have your common sense. I think my biggest fear was, that you would somehow turn away in a direction that I wouldn't be able or willing to do anything with you anymore".

She adds, "You mean, you were worried that I would change and that this would have an impact on our relationship?"

I nod, "Yes, exactly. And there is more. I'm also afraid that there will be some digging around in your childhood to scrutinize where the parents did something wrong. For you to find that I screwed something up. And when you discover that you might be angry at me and don't like me anymore. Is that true? Is that what you're doing there searching for parents' mistakes?"

She answers, "No. I wouldn't call it like that. The aim is not to find mistakes or to judge actions that happened in the past. Instead we search to understand. We want to find the good reasons; people did what they did. The idea is: we cannot change what happened in the past, because it is over. Instead, we look at how we feel now about what we experienced back then. What we need nowadays and what we can do today, so we can find peace for ourselves. Is that scaring?"

I deny, "No. It´s more goal oriented. I like that. And is there something that I have done wrong?"

She says, "Well, we're talking now and it's very valuable to me right now."

I agree, "Yes, also for me. And our conversation is so honest and open. Did you learn that in your seminars as well?"

She answers, "Yes, and also to be courageous to address such matters."

I comment, "Then I like what you are doing ..."

A beautiful moment, I am satisfied, free of fear and worry. All is well. I feel the trust in my daughter, in myself, in our relationship. We are close, dearly close. I have the idea nothing in this world can come between us.

Bathed in this confidence, there is still one more tiny little thing appearing I want to address, "You became such a beautiful woman, really beautiful, and on top of that you have your heart on the right place and you are smart. I wonder why men queuing up before you. I mean, if I were young and would encounter you, I would do everything to be with you. Whenever I ask you how your seminar was, I also want to know if there is someone in your life you allow by your side. That's what I wish for you. Because I've experienced, having a partner on once side, you can achieve so much more, have so much more strength, get so much support and life is simply more beautiful. I wish the same for you. Do you believe me?"

She looks at me and says, "Yes, I believe you. I hear you wish me an easy, beautiful life".

I agree, "Yes, exactly."

She answers, "Okay. I promise I'll let you know, whenever someone comes by my side with whom I can imagine that."

"Thanks.", I say, and we slide out of our roles of the role play.

We walk back to the seminar. She adds, "Fascinating. Last time I visited my dad, he actually asked me about the person at my side."

70

Self-harm

This is a coaching by phone. I received an 'emergency empathy' request in the afternoon and I had time for it in the evening. Guiding someone by phone is always a challenge for me because I can't observe the other person. I lack a lot of information, and whenever pauses occur, I am limited to speech. So, I frequently ask, "What is happening now?" or, "What is going on inside of you?" And still, coaching on the phone is better than no support at all.

I'm talking to the father of a 15-year-old boy. He speaks very fast. His pitch is high, his voice shaky. "My son cut himself horribly in a clearly visible place. It was self-inflicted. He has harmed himself before. I thought he was over it by now and then it happens again. We are now on school vacation and I am about to bring him to my parents' tomorrow. We agreed on this because I have to travel far. There is no way I can cancel that. Hopefully my parents won't see the cuts. I have no idea how they will react when they realize what he did to himself. And even more so my ex-wife. When she is going to get him back from my parents, she will definitely notice. And then all hell breaks loose. Maybe I should call her in advance. But you know how it is in our relationship."

"Yes. I know it's hard for you to trust each other in these days."

"Exactly. She will accuse me by saying it's all my fault, that I've done everything wrong."

"Are you more worried about your son or his mother's reaction to it?" I posed this question to decide what topic we are dealing with.

He says, "More about my son. He spends all day in his room, and I keep telling him to go out to meet friends. The only thing I can get him to do is play the guitar. But I have to persuade him to it. Very docile he will attend his guitar class, but only after I tell him to go. When he returns his mood is always improved."

"Do you have any idea what he is doing in his room?"

"Yeah, he watches videos on YouTube."

"What kind of videos?"

"Well, he is looking for everything that's bad in the world. I told him he also needs to see the positive things in life and that it will depress him if he only watches all the bad things. And I am right, it depresses him."

I respond, "That reminds me of my own daughters. When they were that age, they became vegan. They wanted to have an impact and contribute to making the world a better place. Do you think that's what's going on for your son?"

"Oh, yes, he is vegan, too." In his voice I hear disapproval, worry and maybe even despair.

I offer, "I now feel a kinship with your son, I wonder if I could slide into his role. May I?"

"Yes." He agrees.

72

"Ok, Dad. What do you want to know about me?"

"Are you feeling very bad?"

"Hm. What's very bad? Now that I'm starting to understand what's going on in the world. I'm horrified. No, I am shocked - that's the right word. How is it possible that so many things are going wrong? How can you allow all this to happen to the animals? And then the climate! And the wars. And the refugees! Nobody is taking responsibility. We all live here in luxury at the expense of the poorer countries, and nobody gives a damn. While everybody sees it clearly. I don´t understand that. And I just don´t know what I can do. I feel so small and unimportant, with so little influence, and that´s killing me. That really depresses me. It paralyses me. How am I supposed to deal with all of this for the rest of my life?

"You should also look at the positive side of life. The world is not all bad".

"Sorry, Dad. But your tips aren't helping right now. In the contrary they actually make it worse. How I perceive it, is that you are part of the deniers, those who pretend as if all were well with the world, and I refuse to believe that is really who you are. You are too important to me for that. I want to be able to look up at you."

"That moves me deeply. Then, what would help you?"

"If I would know I´m not standing alone in all of this. If I would hear that you feel exactly the same as I do. Can you tell me that? Well, of course only if it is the truth. How is it for you?"

Pause - long pause, I guess he's struggling with himself. "Phew, not so easy to take in. But, yes. Everything you describe is also inside of me. The powerlessness, helplessness, feeling very small and sometimes also resignation. It feels so awful."

The father sounds different now, his voice has altered, somehow calmer, more honest, credible. I no longer sense his fear or worry, and his words allow me to feel relief.

"Really, you feel the same as me?"

"Yes, it breaks my heart if I allow it to arise."

"Now that's exactly how I feel!" Silence, comforting silence. I am not alone. I am calming down and my dad seems to as well. Then I get curious and ask, "And how do you deal with that?"

"Well, I'm looking for means to make a difference in my everyday life. To act on things I can influence, to make the world a better place. I also celebrate the moments when I see that my contribution made a difference for someone's life. I sort out the garbage and seldom eat meat. I use public transport instead of a car. And I stopped shopping in wholesale markets because there it's so obviously somethings not right. These masses of goods overwhelm me. I am very vigilant for that kind of powerless feelings. So instead I focus my attention on the beautiful things happening in the world and search how I can contribute to them. Maybe that is some kind of denying. Is that pretending all is well in the world for you?"

"Yes, maybe, I don't know. But it's not so important anymore. Now it is assuring to know that I am not standing alone with all those feelings. It helped me a lot to hear that you feel the same way. And it also helps to see that you have ways of dealing with it. Maybe I can find more things that I can do.

Again silence, comforting silence, peaceful, a feeling of "Everything is alright, it's all been said" is spreading between us.

We step out of the role play. The father is relieved, and I add, "If you succeed in opening up like this with your son, magic can happen. Do you think you can be that honest?"

"Yes. I think so," he says, and we end the conversation.

Reading the story to my husband, he asks, "But, what happened with the self-harming behavior?" I answer that it wasn't an issue anymore, it was somehow gone. "I'm really interested in what happens next." My husband adds.

After a week I got the following SMS from the father:
"Dear Gundi, just because you empathized with my son and I was able to hear what might be going on for him, a lot of things simply dissolved into thin air. This week he was in a good mood, laughing, was open minded, frank and even showed me his arm! Thank you so much again".

The acceptance pill

I'm a participant attending a seminar by Kelly Bryson. I like Kelly. His big topic is: Don't give up, give in. Be honest instead of polite, if the relationship is important to you. Don't give yourself up to preserve the relationship but bring yourself in with your truth. This topic is still a learning edge for me. He also has a systemic therapy background and was a student of Virginia Satir. Maybe the acceptance pill comes from there. Unfortunately, I failed to ask him. Anyway, I used this metaphor a couple of times while working with people and I was always amazed about the huge impact of it. Here is the story of my first experience with it. As far as I can remember our task was to think of a situation where you were angry or frustrated or something like that. Find a partner. Tell him or her about your trigger and let him or her give you the acceptance pill. Swallow it and accept whatever life brings you. Accepting also means letting go of the idea that I can change something about it.

That sounded pretty simple to do. In fact, I can't even remember what my topic was back then, only that I worked on it and that it worked damn well. But I can still remember my counterpart very well. He spoke about his son who gets bullied at school. He shared how angry he gets hearing this. How great his urge is to put his son's world back in order and how helpless he feels when he is doomed to watch. His son forbids him to intervene.

I give him the imaginary pill and he swallows it. We wait a while. Apparently, it just takes time until full effect takes place ... and then he says, "So, if I now accept that he gets bullied, it reminds me of myself. I was bullied, too."

"And?" I ask.

"Well, actually it wasn't that bad. I mean, it was hard at the moment it happened, but I also learned a lot from it."

"Really? Like what?", I ask.

"Well, to defend myself, and also not to take everything so personal and to put on a protective coat and finally to become strong and not to let myself be hurt by what is brought to me from outside. Oh yes, also to ask for help when I can't cope it any longer, and even to accept that help."

Wow. That is a big change.

I always want to be there for you

Another 9-day intensive seminar. A private session. We are outside strolling. Somehow, I have the impression that walking supports a process. When we walk, the topic is also moving forward. Sometimes fast and sometimes slow and sometimes it even needs a break or a stop for a moment, maybe even a look back over the shoulder.

We walk next to each other and she shares, "I have a five-year-old daughter". Her eyes start to shine, she smiles. My heart gets warm from all the love that suddenly appeared. She tells me how valuable the little one is to her. How beautiful their relationship is and how happy she is to have NVC as a tool that makes this kind of relationship so much easier. We bathe for a while in the preciousness and gratitude for all this.

Then I get curious and ask, "Was that it? Did you only want to celebrate with me what life gives you, or is there something else?"

She adds, "Well, I can't get on an airplane".

I don't quite understand and ask, "Tell me more!"

She says, "I can't get on a plane, because I'm afraid something will happen to me and my daughter will be alone. Flying is not an option for me! I was also afraid to come here - the long drive with the car, something could have happened to me, and then ..."

"And then what?" I ask carefully.

"Then my daughter would miss out on everything I still want to give her."

"And then?" I ask.

"That would be so bad, I can't even think about it."

I realize that she is not ready to look at her worst fears in this moment. I am in awe and I have great respect for humankind, for all the resources and protective mechanisms at our disposal. I decide to tag along. "I hear that what you can give her is unique, valuable and precious and that you wish to give her this quality of togetherness for as long as possible."

She stops and looks at me. "Yes", she acknowledges. Tears well up from her eyes and slowly find their way down her cheeks, silent tears, packed with emotion and longing. We stand still for a while. Then she continues to walk, slowly, step by step. I tag along in utter silence.

After a while, I ask, "With whom is your daughter now?

"With my husband and with my mom."

"Does she like being there?"

"Yes. My husband is a great dad. He spends time with her and is also very patient with her. Besides, they now do things they wouldn't do when I'm around".

"Sounds as if you could let go confidently, knowing that the two are doing well together?"

"Yes."

"And with your mom, how is your daughter doing with her grandma?"

"Very good. They match well also. Ok, my mom doesn't give her the space I give her to experience feelings. My daughter is allowed to be sad when she is with me. My mom can't stand her being sad, she then tries to comfort her immediately, but that's okay. My daughter can live that out with me."

"It seems to be very important for you that she experiences all of her feelings to be welcome?"

"Yes".

"And is her Dad able to do that?"

"He's improving quite well."

Somehow, in this conversation, I am under the impression that we keep spinning in a circle, there is hardly any energy left. We got stuck, and I address it. She feels the same way.

"Is there anything else with your mom?", I ask.

"I also have a wonderful relationship with my mom and dad. They are still very important people in my life. I wish for my little one that I am *always* there for her, too".

Something about the pronunciation of the word "always" makes me wonder. "Always?", I ask.

"Yes, always."

I think about it for a while... "That implies that your little one would have to leave this earth before you."

She thinks about it... "No, I do not want that to happen!"

80

The acceptance pill comes into mind. I have a few almonds in the pocket of my jacket. I take one out and present it with the words, "This is an acceptance pill. If you swallow it, you will accept the things you cannot change. You will accept, that you have no influence on some things. Do you want to try it?"

The almond is presented on my outstretched hand. I offer it to her. She looks at it. Again, soft tears well up from her eyes. She looks as if she is struggling with herself. Eventually she grabs the almond, puts it in her mouth and starts to chew. More tears appear. I don't think I've ever before, watched another person chewing an almond with so much curiosity. I am so curious about what is going to happen next. I am also grateful for the trust bestowed on me. It is like a holy moment. After a long silence the tears stop. She starts to walk again. I follow. And for at least five minutes in silence, I indulge in the deep confidence that something nurturing is happening.

Finally, she starts sharing the story of her friends, who were also parents. The mother died early, and the father quit working in order to be there for their son. Eventually it all worked out. They made it. Actually, they made it quite well. "I think my husband would make it as well. My parents are also still present and would support him fully. He would not even have to quit working. We live close to each other. My mother could take care for my daughter after school, and my husband could pick her up there after work. That would work fine."

There is no trace of fear left in her voice, only hope, confidence and trust.

What a magical almond.

I did the right thing

A workshop on Restorative Circles. They are related to the NVC. The main idea is: In order to resolve conflicts all participants come together. They sit in circles, meet each other as equals and make space to hear the truths as everyone has experienced. Everyone gets to share whatever needs to be said, unfiltered including the allegations. Then the speaker chooses who he or she wants to repeat what's understood. The sender of the message checks whether that really is what he or she wants to communicate. When everything has been said and heard, the joint solution search commences. In my experience this is a process with enormous potential for healing. (More information about Restorative Circles at www.restorativecircles.com.)

We practice. One participant wants to tell her mother how much she suffered from her mother's passively letting it happen while her father used massive physical violence against the both of them. I step into the role of the mother. My daughter accuses me. She screams, "How could you just watch passively in all these years? Why didn't you help me?"

I freeze, stiff like a plank, immobilized. My thoughts are razor sharp clear. I did the right thing. I would do exactly the same thing again today. I am absolutely sure about it. It is the only way. I have thought carefully about all the possibilities.

There is no alternative. This is the only way to survive. Hold tight, wait motionless until it's over. When it started, I always hoped in silence: Please pick me instead of the girl. I can cope with it. And when he picked the girl, I prayed silently to her, "Please hold still, hold on! Just wait until it's over. Just don't provoke him. Don't do anything unexpected. That only makes him angrier."

That is what I tell my daughter from my role in the roleplay. She cries and finally says, "It was so hard for me". She wants me to repeat that.

I see her. She cries. I'm sorry in my head, but I can't feel a thing. I can't get through, not to me, because it's so clear to me: We are alive. The both of us are. We both survived. That is what counts. I made that possible. This is why I am so convinced, that I did the right thing. That is all I can say, there is nothing more to it.

She wants me to repeat her words. I can do that. "It was hard for you." It was easy to repeat that, because it was the same for me. But I learned to live with it. Holding still and waiting it out. It is just physical pain and the wounds will heal anyhow, just as the sun comes out after the rain and the day returns after the night.

As Gundi I was surprised and even shocked after this role play. I rarely experience such clarity from within myself. Only when it comes to letting my three-year-old child play on the motorway or not. Then I have a similar clarity. What remains for me is the question: Is it true what I experienced there? Does that happen to a person who watches her child get beaten or something along that line?

Anyhow, the daughter said that the roleplay was helpful to her. She got a rare insight into her mother's world and that provided a little healing.

I also got feedback from a befriended trainer who was observing. He was really in rage when he told me, "I could hardly believe what came out of your mouth. I was horrified, outraged, really angry. I just wanted to grab you, shake you and yell at you, 'Do take responsibility and defend yourself and most of all: Protect your child! That's your damned duty as a mother!'"

Yes. I probably would have had the same reaction, if I were in his shoes.

The shame

A nine-day training in NVC. My husband Frank is present as a trainer, I am attending as a participant. During the break he asks me and another trainer if we are willing to take on the roles of two five-year-old children, who fought over a ball. He wants to announce his workshop "Mediation with children" in a vivid way by means of a short demo. We were very willing to play along!

The moment had come. Everyone was present: All trainers, all participants, all organizers, about fifty people. All gathered in our big room. A large circle of chairs has been set up and many chairs are occupied. In addition, there were cushions in the middle and some people were sitting and lying, some of them cuddling. At such events community is forged, and people get close. I also sit on the floor among other participants, who have become very familiar to me. It is the penultimate day. I am crocheting comfortably and waiting for my turn. My teammate is sitting on an opposite chair at the other end of the room. Frank gets up and says in a loud, sharp voice, "GUNDI!" He says it in a very special tone, that is incredibly difficult for me to describe. But the effect is nevertheless unstoppable frightening. My whole body is in state of high alert. I duck and try to hide behind others' backs. I know very well that 'I did something wrong' and that I am now being summoned to account. I am afraid. Then I hear his voice again. This time louder and even more demanding, "GUNDI! STAND UP!" In-stinctively I make myself smaller, trying to be un-noticeable behind the back of the man before me. He sensed it and makes himself bigger, wider, providing cover. One voice inside me screams, "Oh my God, don't get up! Just hide. Just pretend you're not here." Another voice in me screams, "Get up! If you don't get up now, it'll only get worse." Torn between these two voices my body reacts. My upper body straightens up a little, only to bend down again immediately. A fight rages in-side of me. And again, I hear his voice, even louder, even sharper, "GUNDI! STAND UP!" Slowly, very slowly, battered by curves, I start to rise. It costs me an incredible amount of strength until I finally stand up. Eyes down, shoulders hanging forward, I feel a stretch in my neck.

And now the fear dissolves and makes way for another feeling. Now that I am standing, every-body can utterly see me. Everybody can see what a bad person I am. A feeling of shame comes over me until it is almost unbearable. Everyone can see me, and everyone can judge me because I did some-thing bad, because I was evil. I hear his voice again, "Peter! Get up!"

Phew. That feels good. I'm not the only one, who was bad. What a relief! Peter gets up. He stands up straight. His feet are wide apart. He is standing tall, crosses his arms in front of his chest and says loudly and clearly, "I didn't do anything! It wasn't me!"

Then Frank turns into the usual Frank again and announces his workshop about supporting children, when there is a fight about a red ball or something similar. I can finally shake off my role and it takes a while until I really get rid of it. It was meant to be just a playful seminar announcement. And yet I did experience everything, and I did feel all these feelings in a very intense way. Other participants are partly confused, some even shocked, "Was that real?"

For me, it was real. I felt everything, unfiltered: first the fear, then the inner conflict, the shame, briefly the hope followed by the envy and finally the indignation, "Why does the other one deny all this? Why can he stand up so straight? And why can't I?"

As Gundi it shocked me. I don't remember that I ever experienced such feelings in my real life. Probably I did sometime, otherwise I could not experience it as intensively as happened just now. I don't know. I probably will not be able to find an answer to this question.

Feeling the fear was kind of ok - I could deal with it. But the shame was horrible, almost unendurable. Having to stand up in front of everyone. To be seen by everyone. Nobody's supposed to go through something like this. Nobody is supposed to feel this shame. I really pray that I will never do something that leads another person to experiencing this. And, in case I can't prevent it that I have the courage to stand up and respond to it with everything at my disposal.

The little boy in the supermarket

The other day at the supermarket, I saw a five years old boy. He climbed around the front of the shopping cart. His father pushed the cart and summoned him to stop. Of course, he didn´t. He just had to much fun.

The inevitable happened, father's prophecy came true. The boy fell down and started crying loudly. His eyes wide open, he looked frightened with a little lost expression on his face. He looked around, searchingly. I knew that his world, which was intact a moment ago, suddenly got destroyed. He needed support from someone to accompany him in bringing his world back in order.

Father's answer came promptly and as expected, "You see, I told you so!"

I hesitated for a moment with the question, "Is it okay for me to interfere here?", but then I followed my heart. I went to the boy, bent down to him to be on the same level and spoke, "That must have been very scary. You were just climbing around the cart so well, having fun in exploring what you can do and probably you were proud of how good you manage to climb. And then: Whoops. All of a sudden you were lying on the floor. Phew, how strange must that be? If that would have happened to me, I would be really shocked. Are you shocked, too?"

He looks at me, stops crying, his gaze becomes clear and awake, and I read something like gratitude in it - at least I interpreted that into it. Then he smiles at me, turns around and marches off.

My gaze goes to the father with the question in my heart, "Have I just crossed your borders?" He looks relaxed. That is enough for me.

Shortly before the cash desk we meet again - he waves, I wave back.

The red ball battle

We are in the workshop "Mediation with children", that was announced in the previous story ("The shame"). Frank makes a demonstration. He is the mediator. I am in the role of five-year-old Katja and another participant is sitting opposite to me. She is in the role of my friend Marta. We assume, that in our kindergarten NVC was introduced by the project "The Giraffe's dream". Me and Marta had a struggle about the red ball. Now we are sitting in the giraffe corner - this is the place we have created to meet each other and clarify things. Frank is supporting us.

Frank, "Thank you for willingness to be here and for trying to solve the struggle between the two of you. I am happy to support you in finding a solution. I will make sure that each of you can say everything important, so that each of you will be heard. Who wants to start?" I hesitate, "Am I really allowed to say everything?" Frank, "Yes, I'll make sure of that." I say, "Okay, let her start then."

Frank gives her the talking stick and me the giraffe ears. Frank, "Marta, what exactly did you see?" Marta addresses me, "You came up to me and pulled the ball out of my hands, and then you pushed me too." Frank to me, "Please tell me what you heard from Marta." I say, "I heard, that I took the ball away from her and pushed her." Frank to me, "Thank you." To Marta, "Did she hear it right?" Marta, "Yes."

Frank, "And what did you see, Katja?" "I played with the ball, and then I had to pee, and when I came back, you had the ball, and then I got it back."

Frank to Marta, "Please say what you've heard from Katja". Marta, "She was in the bathroom and when she came back, I had the ball and then she took it back." Frank to me, "Did she hear you correctly?" "Yes."

Frank to me, "And how do you feel now?" I'm still thinking and searching for my feelings when Marta says, "Are you sad, too?" "Yes."" Frank, "And what do you need now?" "That we are friends again". Marta, "I want that, too!"

Frank, "Do you have any idea what you want to do now?" Marta, "I was so happy before that the other group of our kindergarten went on a road trip today, and that I finally got the chance to play with that great red ball, because when they are here, they always have the ball." I, "I can help you and together we can make sure the others don't get the ball". Marta, "Yes, and if you have to pee, I'll come along with you and we'll take the ball with us to the toilet."

Great solution for us children! We are done. Problem solved.

Frank, "Wow. I so much enjoyed this, how the two of you managed to find a solution for your struggle. I would like everyone to learn from it. Are you two willing to share this experience in the morning circle tomorrow?"

Again, and again I am amazed of how easy and quick this process works with children. Maybe because they live much more in the "now"? Enviable! Mediations with adults take much longer.

There are some helpful aspects hidden in the process, that I would like to discuss. In the beginning Frank thanked us and made it clear that he is happy to support us. This took away some of my fear for punishment and scolding. I was aware what I did was not okay. So, no need to rub that in! I was still a bit skeptic, but his words made it easier for me to remain present. It was definitely not a comfortable place to be, but I could live with it.

Then he said that he would make sure really every one of us could say everything. He even repeated it. That helped me to gain trust and listen to my friend first. Otherwise I would have wanted to be the first one to make sure that my side of the story was heard.

The next step: To repeat what Marta said was kind of annoying, but not really difficult, because there was no accusation in it. She didn't say that I did something bad or wrong.

Then Frank asked, "What did you see? It was a clear question. I just tried to describe again from my point of view what I saw. That was easy to answer and didn't trigger any big emotions in me either.

On the other hand, a question like, "What happened?" would have triggered me to revisit the drama as I experienced it before. All injustice would have revolved back into the room. I would have bathed in my role as the victim. I would have searched for the reason of my misery and Marta would take all the blame for it. If I told my version of what happened, it would become the truth as I see it. And then, she would have told her truth and we would fight over what truth is right. That just doesn´t serve resolving the conflict. It doesn´t lead to resolutions. The powder would be shot before we reached the core, if we even would reach it at all. Because once I took on my victim role, I need compassion and confirmation and will first try to make the mediator a judge to pull him to my side. It won't take long before I sit on his lap and look at him with big, expectant puppy eyes and maybe even shed a tear. That strategy always works - at least it's the best thing I can think of. That's what I've learned.

Instead of that, we remained on the level of pure observation. And even if she saw something different than me, it would not be a threat.

Franks following question was, "How do you feel now?" instead of, "How did you feel in the situation?" Now we're sitting here, and I heard something from her that I didn't know before and she heard my side in return. So now, I feel different than in the situation back then. When the focus is on how I felt back then, my anger is triggered, and it will definitely pop up. But now is now and it´s different. Going back in past experiences might be tremendous helpful in therapy work, when the client declares, "I want to learn new patterns of behavior to deal with my anger". But we are in the giraffe corner in the kindergarten and want to solve a conflict and not hold a therapy session. Here we are normally accompanied either by an educator or another child and no therapist.

One more thing to add to the question, "How do you feel now". I have often been in the role of a child. Again, and again I experienced magic. When the feelings are expressed, understanding happens. With adults, this 'Herzspitzenberührung' (Heart-Touchings) usually happen, when we hear each other's needs in their beauty and truly understand each other. Interesting. I don't have an explanation for that, I don´t know why, (yet).

Another aspect: In the child´s role, it helped me a lot that Marta offered me the feeling 'sad' along with the word 'also'. While I was still searching for my feeling, she offered me one and I realized, that was it. Plus, she revealed a little bit of herself. That made it so easy for me to say "yes". It was true. I was sad and hearing this little word, 'also', helped me to tell my truth. It seemed to be okay to say it, and I dared to do it.

The question, "What do you need now?" was also very clear and super easy to answer. I knew she wanted exactly the same.

In the end Frank thanked us. I liked that. I felt great. My doing brought a little joy to him. My pleasure, Frank!

And finally, Frank asked us if we are willing to share this with everybody in the morning circle, because he wants everyone to learn from it. I also liked that. I'm proud and important. I did the right thing and now I'm teaching it to everyone else, because now I know how it works. Maybe we will skip a little part of the solutions that we found, because tomorrow the others will be back from the excursion and after all, Marta and I want to play with the 'red ball' by ourselves.

Experiences in "real life"

But I want to join my yoga class

Every Tuesday I attend yoga class. It's really nurturing for me and I'm proud I manage to attend so consistently. It is an offering from my employer. Usually I sign up in the google list in the morning. Since I drive by car from work to the gym, I offer a ride for three more people. Usually I drive up to the pick-up point around 2.25 pm, where mostly between two and three girls wait for the ride.

This day a meeting was postponed, and I was unsure if I would made it in time, so I didn't register. But it worked out. The meeting was finished in time and I could leave on time. The walk to my car leads past long haul coaches. The bus station is around the corner and buses from Eastern Europe usually park in this street.

I was born in Romania and somehow these buses remind me of my first home. It still holds a warm space in my heart since I have beautiful memories of my life of the village, I grew up in. I am walking past a bus, wondering where it comes from when I see a man. He looks Eastern European, dark hair, dark eyes and a few teeth are missing. I guess he's a little older than me and probably the bus driver. I'm just wondering what his life would be like. Our eyes intersect, we both smile and greet another. He waits a little and then asks me something. He speaks broken German, only a few words. Something with "parking" and "tomorrow evening". Then he goes to another bus and points to the parking disc, which is clearly visible in the window. "Where buy?" Obviously, he needs a parking disc. I have three in my car and I instruct him to follow me. *A voice in my brain starts commentating, "It could work out in time. I'll just give him the parking disc and I can still make it in time for yoga!"*

We get to my car. I give him the disc, he thanks me and then he keeps looking at me. He looks at me with these big lost eyes, and I realize that he doesn't know what to do with it.

My inner voice interferes again, *"Shit. The only thing I know is that you have to present the parking disc from 9.00 a.m. (if you certainly don't want a parking ticket), and that it's valid for four hours. When I park my car there, I get back there before 13 o'clock and adjust it. That works fine for me. I don't have any clue in which timeframe the parking disc must be presented. What I do know, is that this information is written on the traffic sign at the beginning of the road. It's a long road! Too far away to make it to the yoga in time! Damn!"*

It's getting tense and I am torn. I try to explain very quickly to him, that at the beginning of the road is a traffic sign with all the information that he needs. He does not understand. Of course not!

I turn around searching for help. There is a man walking over there. I point my finger at him and say: Maybe he can help you? But that walking man moves away from us. The bus driver still looks at me with big eyes.

"Okay. Now it's time for a decision! I glance at the pick-up meeting point. Nobody there. Okay. Good. That relieves me and gives me some space. If I get to yoga class too late, I will miss the initial relaxation. It's a pity, but doable. I just arrive there a little later and I can look through the window when they start stretching. The perfect moment to join the class without disturbing anybody. The most important thing is the relaxation at the end anyhow! And this man, right in front of me needs support. So, I decide to take the time for him now!"

We go to the road sign, and I'm surprised. It was less far than expected. Over there I calmly explain him how it works with the four hours. I use all my assets, body, I make big gestures, count with my fingers. And slowly, he starts to understand, to nod his head, to count with his fingers and to turn the parking disc to proof he understood: The parking disc must be clearly visible in the bus until 6 p.m. and then again from 9 a.m. the next morning. I agree. His eyes shine now. He looks proud. He understood. I am proud. It actually worked, with hands and feet and a lot of patience I explained it to him, and now he knows and seems to be so happy.

So, we go back to my car and he says he would like to invite me for a cup of coffee. I say, "Next time, because I want to go to my yoga class." We almost reached my car, when he suddenly stops and says, "You must come. I give you". He says it in a very straight way and this time I understand that it's precious. It is so obvious and clear to me that I will go with him. No more doubts and I think, *"If I miss yoga today, it's okay."* We pass my car and I follow him to his bus. He says, "My daughter live Mannheim. My wife says: Go Frankfurt and bring things to daughter. But no go. I give you". We reach his bus. He enters and comes out again with a bag. It is brim full and can barely stand by itself. A small plastic bag lies on top. He removes it - maybe his sandwich? Now I see courgettis, big and small ones, eggplants and an aluminum foil. He takes the foil out and reveals its preciousness very proudly: huge cloves of garlic. I am thrilled, "Ohhhh, so big and beautiful vegetables."

He says, "Yesterday in garden, today here, nothing a week, yesterday. My wife and other daughter in Bosnia!"

And now I can visualize them: the mother, how she reaps the most beautiful things from her garden together with the sister. How they lovingly pack all the treasures for the daughter and sister that lives far away in a foreign country. I can see how they add all their love to these vegetables. And now I'm supposed to receive all that ... it moves me deeply and tears appear. All that love. I tell him, "Oh, so much love is in it! From Mom and sister." He embraces me and says, "I carry bag!" He accompanies me to the car, loads in the treasures and I drive off. It is 2.45 p.m. and I arrive in the changing room at 2.55 p.m. where I meet Diana, my colleague. I am so overwhelmed of what I have just experienced that it all bubbles out of me. She listens to me and in the end, she says, "Well then you are in just the right mood for yoga!" How true! We open the door and enter. We are on time, so punctual!

Tabea is drawing

We are on holiday. I am sitting in a hotel lobby. Next to me, a little girl is drawing a picture. We already had a little contact. I told her my name and she said, "My name is Tabea." I told her I am waiting here for my girls, and she told me that she is drawing. She is completely absorbed in her doing and I am fascinated by it. Every once in a while, she interrupts her drawing, looks at the picture, looks at her pencils, chooses a new color and continues drawing. Now she is finished. She walks up to me, hands me her picture and says, "Here, for you".

I'm happy. Even more, I am very excited. And I wonder why? What exactly is it that causes these beautiful feelings inside of me? So, I'm starting to search inward and discover a whole bunch of flowers of fulfilled needs.

I tell her, "A gift. For me? Oh, I feel honored, because you only give something to someone you like, and now I think that you like me. Is that true?"

She pulls up her right shoulder and tilts her head towards it, so that her ear almost touches her shoulder and she smiles.

"Also, I see that you used blue, red, yellow and purple in your picture. That is quite colorful, and I like colorful very much. Look, my dress is also quite colorful!

Now she swings back and forth on her legs.

"Uh, and I watched you drawing, and then you stopped and looked at all your pencils and then selected a color. I assume, that you took your time to think about, what color would be beautiful next and also about what else is needed on the picture. Is that true?"

She says, "Hmmh" and her head goes up and down in big nodding movements.

"I also like taking my time to choose what would be beautiful." Now it seems like we are both surfing on a wave of enjoying aesthetics.

Something more appears inside of me, "And there is something else I really enjoyed. It seemed to me, that it felt so good for you, when you gave me your picture as a present. For me, giving presents is also great. It feels so good to give somebody a gift. And it feels so good to receive one also. Giving makes everyone happy, both the giver and the receiver. I think that's great. You too?

Again, I get a huge nod.

"Do you also want to draw a picture?" she asks me. "Then you can also give it away."

Yes, I want to. What a nice idea.

And then we both draw, immerse ourselves in the world of colors and shapes, where nothing else matters.

Unconditional love in a tea mug

Another nine-day training. We arrived two days before, so that the trainers have enough time for preparation. My husband Frank is attending as a trainer, I as a participant. We are accommodated with the other two trainers in a "chalet". It deserves that name, it's really fabulous. Lovingly furnished in the style of an English mansion with a view at the lake and a cozy fireplace in the living room, a fancy modern and fully equipped kitchen, which had to be handmade tailored by a carpenter. Even a vegetable peeler is present. And of course, cups. The three trainers are meeting in preparation for the seminar. I have got time, since I am on vacation, and snoop around in the kitchen. I'm already looking forward to all the intensive encounters that lie ahead of me. My heart is already much more open than in my normal everyday life. One of the trainers appears in the kitchen. He wants to poor himself tea. He carries a normal sized cup in his hand and puts two tea bags in it. I get curious. When I prepare tea, I use one bag for a whole pot. So, I ask him about it. He tells me, that he loves to drink tea from a big mug and that he already scrutinized the whole kitchen, and this is the biggest cup provided. There is a bigger one, meant for measuring liquids, but that wasn't suitable to drink tea from. He pours the hot water into his cup and goes back into the living room.

My heart gets warm. I've just received a little treasure about him. Something I can make him happy with. I would love to find a big mug to make his life more wonderful. I search through all the cupboards and drawers again, without result.

A little later I went shopping to pass the time and buy some snacks for everyone. In the supermarket I caught myself looking for a big mug. But, no mugs. Too bad - it would have been nice.

Back in our car, my gaze falls on the footwell of the passenger seat. There is my cereal bowl. I suddenly recall our departure the day before. It was hectic. I prepared myself some cereal and didn't get to finish eating it at home. So, I took it along into the car and ate it in peace and quiet, while my husband was driving.

This cereal bowl can serve perfectly as a big tea mug. It even has a funny face on it. I get all excited and happy by that thought. So much warmth and joyful power spreads over my whole body and I can hardly wait, to see him, when I offer him my bowl. I imagine, how his eyes will radiate and how he will start to smile and how happy he will be.

Imagining this, pure joy fills me up, the childlike real kind of joy. My heart almost explodes from all the love I have inside of me. So much energy, life and warmth. I imagine, that every time he drinks tea from it, he will get happy. With this life inside me, I float back to our chalet with an ear to ear smile. When I enter the house, I find them busy, completely absorbed into their work. I don't want to disturb them. I am a little disappointed and park my joy. I place the mug on a table in the corner and write a note. "For you from the heart. Enjoy it."

Days are passing - at such seminars a lot happens in a short time - and I had almost forgotten about the bowl when I fetched something from our chalet. I'm on my way out again, when he calls me, "I wanted to thank you for the mug. I was so happy." I reply, "Oh, beautiful", and leave, since I am in a hurry. I want to be at the Seminar on time. After a few steps outside, I pause for a moment. I notice, that there is more to be said, turn around, go back and add, "It really came from the heart". He smiles. I turn around again and move on to my "important appointment". While I am walking out, I kindly remember the situation, when I saw my cereal bowl in our car and these warm feelings appear again. I realize, that there is so much more to share about my joy, but definitely not now. The days pass and on the last day of the training the opportunity actually arises. My "tea mug trainer" offers a workshop on "appreciation", and I attend it. We are all sitting in a fictitious waiting room with an invitation to think about who we want to tell that he or she has enriched our lives.

The invitation was to fetch the person, to look for a cozy place and tell him or her, how they have enriched our lives, by telling them what they did actually, what feelings that triggered in us and what needs were fulfilled by that. Now was my time to share it all. I picked him, and we went into a corner.

When I was finally sitting towards him, I got so incredibly excited I trembled. What was going on? I got shaky and I was really surprised about my body reaction. Why am I shaking, when I am ready to tell someone something so beautiful?

I decided to kindly park my confusion, since I really wanted to share my whole truth. I told him, how much love appeared in my heart when I found the bowl and how joyful it was for me to imagine him being happy to receive my gift. I told him, how damn good that felt.

Then he shared his side: It was precious for him to find the big mug with the note. Very precious. In a special way. For him it was like, someone gave this gift to him, really meaning to nurture him. Really meant for him. For him, at the core of his being. Not the trainer or the father or the partner or any role he takes on, but for him.

Hearing that, touched a very deep place in my heart. That was exactly how I meant it, exactly my intention. And he received it exactly like that. I wanted to bring joy to this beautiful soul. It was particularly valuable because, he not only gave me the pleasure to give him this pleasure, but also that the quality of my intention was seen, and moreover, that it nurtured a deep longing in him. While I am writing this, these beautiful feelings raise again. Over and over I am bathing in unconditional love.

Oh, and I wonder why I was so churned up, in the moment I chose to tell him my truth. Perhaps, because I felt this pure quality of love in me so intensely. Sharing this preciousness has also made me vulnerable. I wonder, if this is the reason why appreciation is so often not expressed: Because it makes us vulnerable?

Experiences in our family

The coffee cup

Friday morning. My husband is off to a seminar. I go into the kitchen and see his coffee cup. It is standing on the top of the dishwasher. I need to repeat this: It's right on the top of it! Gosh! I'm annoyed. It's AGAIN on top of it! Really?! Why can't he just do what I asked him to? Is it really too much to ask for? Is it so hard to put his bloody cup INSIDE the dishwasher? I told him so many times and we recently discussed this matter extensively. I even used the four steps of NVC. I told him my needs: Order and support! Why doesn't it work? This whole NVC stuff is useless… Is that true?

Maybe I could give it just one more try? One more! Ok! I choose to go on another exploration journey to find out what needs are underneath "order" and "support".

A friend of mine, Lorna Ritchie, shared a very helpful metaphor with me: An emphatic journey is like peeling an onion. You can remove it layer by layer by continuing asking, "What is fulfilled, if I get …(need)?" When judgments appear, you look for their opposites in order to find the need behind.

Then the next layer appears, and you can repeat the process. While peeling the onion, you might shed a few tears, until you reach its sweet core.

I start to peel. When everything is in its right place, just the way I like it and "my" order is fulfilled… Warm feelings arise in my stomach area. I take a deep breath and exhale. Then it's nice at home. I can finally come to rest. If everything is in the way I like it, I can finally sit down and relax. Then I finally have time for myself. Now I am calmer, and a pleasant feeling fills me. That is exactly what I want to tell him the next time we discuss this.

Now another thought appears, "AGAIN. He did it again. We discussed this, he knows what I want, and he did it again." I focus on my body and notice how my shoulders drop and tiredness and exhaustion are spreading. "I've told him so many times." - Yes, I want to be heard. But he heard me! He even repeated it. Quite well-behaved, completely by the book. So, why doesn´t he do it? Why doesn´t he walk his talk? What withholds him from doing this tiny little thingy for me?

That reminds me of the saying of Marshall B. Rosenberg, which I find very valuable. I even laminated it and put it on our front door as a constant reminder, "Everything we do is the best and most beautiful thing we can think of to meet our needs."

So, which need of my husband is fulfilled by leaving the cup on top and ignore my request. It must be something very precious. I get curious and decide to ask him exactly that.

What remains now, is a certain doubt: Am I still important to him? Do I count for him? Do I have a place in his heart? And while I seriously ask myself this questions, various moments experienced together come to my mind. No, I don't need to question that part. The coffee cup on the dishwasher is really not the right calibrated measuring instrument for answering this question! Phew, thank God - I am relieved.

We take our time for the conversation. I share my discoveries and insights with him, and he is also willing to investigate his side. We go on the journey together and discover the "yes" behind his "no". The precious needs that kept him from fulfilling my request.

Unconsciously he is marking his territory with traces when he leaves the house, to show that he is still present, that he has his place in our common home. Experiencing this, moves me and changes something in me. He is often gone actually. So, I ask him to leave the cup on top from now, because it now has a new meaning for me: It is a reminder that he exists in my life, even when he is on the road. And I am grateful for that. Now I can sit down relaxed in my armchair, and when I see the coffee cup, he is somehow present with me and I am happy and grateful for that.

And whenever this picture triggers a rumbling in me, I now see it as a hint to take care of the relationship and either to explore whether something calls to be clarified or simply to do something beautiful together that nourishes our relationship.

Why tidy up rooms

Classical topics of conflict. They pop up very often in parent training sessions and we have also experienced them ourselves. They are "going to bed", "brushing teeth", "getting out of the house on time in the morning", "doing homework", "tidying up the room", "taking out the garbage", "the use of mobile phones, tablets, television and computers".

One of my own first main topics with my children was "Cleaning the room". I enter my daughter's room and see several pieces of clothing, pens and drawings lying on the floor. That would be the first step: The observation. It beats thoughts like, "What a pigsty!" Instead, pointing out the concrete facts will defuse some tension.

When there are clothes on the floor, I am …. The challenge starts: What am I? What do I feel?

I invite you to take that journey and find your own feeling. What does that observation trigger in you? Are you angry, irritated, disappointed, frustrated? For me it was something between annoyed and angry.

The next step is to find out what's your need behind your feeling. What is it really about? What is missing or not fulfilled? Is it about order?

For me, order was spot on, at least on the top level. I can go on by asking: Is it true? Am I really concerned about order? Ah, there is the onion again: the outermost layer is order. When it is removed, a deeper layer emerges. The question that leads to this deeper layer is: What is fulfilled for me when I get order?

What is fulfilled for you?

I uncovered: Then I feel comfortable in my home. I can finally relax, rest, recharge, just like what I discovered in my example with the coffee cup. Yes, that feels good, that's what I long for.

And at the same time, there must be more to it, because I could just close the door of her room and sit down in my comfortable armchair. The search continues. What else do I need? Something whirls up, like "passing on values": I would like to pass on my precious, helpful experiences. All the things that made my life beautiful and easy. At this point, my husband comes to my mind, who lives a completely different understanding of order and, surprisingly enough, gets along quite well with his life.

Aha, again something new pops up. I would like my daughter to get through life easily. That opens another door for me. My focus shifts to all the things she already learned, and I realize that she already has a vast amount of resources at her disposal. As my trust in her grows, I can let go a little bit more now. It doesn't seem so important anymore that she chooses to follow exactly my principles of order. My anger completely evaporated. Instead it made room to bathe in trust and lightness. In this energy I can now approach her and share my insights. Together we can celebrate how beautiful it is for me when the floor is empty, how comfortable it makes me feel, how easily I can find things when they are always exactly where they belong. And: That I have just opened up a little bit more for other concepts of life and order. Because, when things are on the floor, it is even easier to find them.

Now you might wonder: But what will happen to the room? Does that mean I have to live with her room not being tidy?

No. My acceptance threshold just went up. But there is still a threshold: My limit! It levels with my energy balance at that moment and can therefore vary. When this limit is exceeded, I really need something to happen. It tripped the alarm to inform people what is going on for me. My daughter was eager to know when I am about to reach this limit. In that case she sometimes cleaned up and other times we spend some time together. Because often when I am about to reach this limit, I am entangled in my own judgments about others and even about myself. What I really need at that moment is contact, proximity, understanding, maybe even some help.

My anger has now transformed into a warning signal for me, an alarm clock that says: Hello-ow! You are in need now! You are stuck in your head and need to reconnect to that what is really important to you. With this new purpose of "anger" it is so much easier for me to take my time and search for what is really going on with me.

The master's degree in hiding anger

This story goes back to the time our daughters were about 12 and 9. We just moved into our new house and back then, the kitchen was in a small room. I had the habit of putting a chair in the corner as an open invitation, as a calling sign, saying: I'm still here for you, even though I'm cooking. Please take a seat and keep me company! The problem with the chair was, it was always in my back whenever I was cooking. If someone happened to sit on it, I always had to turn around in order to have eye contact. I don't really enjoy cooking all by myself. I prefer someone to be there with me. Not necessarily to help, just to have company.

That day I was standing in the kitchen, stirring in my cooking pot and facing the wall. Frank was off somewhere on some seminar. The day was pretty exhausting so far and I was standing there all by myself. I was annoyed and entangled in a familiar mood that told me something like, "I always have to do everything alone", when my older daughter came into the kitchen and sat down on the chair behind me. She observed me for a while and then asked, "Is everything okay?"

"Sure!" I replied.

"Are you sure?"

"Yes."

Somehow, I had the impression from NVC that it's not appropriate to be angry, especially not for a certified trainer. I also understood that anger is only derived from my "wrong" thoughts and that it is my responsibility to transform these thoughts in a self-empathy process to get rid of my anger. To remain in this process until the anger is eventually transformed into beautiful life supporting needs. To continue until all the "negative" energy left and all the blame or criticism in my heart vanished. That worked well in seminars having the right setting, enough rest, plenty of time and guidance from the trainer or support from an empathy body. But in everyday life that process of self-empathy was quiet challenging and sometimes I still got stuck in my anger or thoughts like, "I am such a victim". By all means I wanted to avoid projecting that anger onto the children. I was worried that I would overwhelm them with my anger that it would harm them and that this would damage our relationship.

So, I chose to remain mute and ignored my anger, buried it. I also felt ashamed because I knew what to do theoretically, but in that moment I did not succeed. Additionally, I failed.

"You look like you're upset!" my daughter continued.

My mind was racing. Damn it, she insists. How do I get out of this one?

"What makes you think that?" I asked and turned to her.

She looked relaxed and said, "Well, when you get angry your face turns red, your gaze narrows, you have a furrow between your eyebrows, you bite your teeth together and breathe faster."

Damn, busted. I was stunned and curious and I said, "How long have you known this?"

"Well, I always have."

Oh, my God, I thought I was a master at hiding that feeling. Then my younger daughter appeared. I asked her, "Do you sometimes notice that I get angry even when I don't say it?"

"Sure."

"How do you know?"

Immediately she says, "You get a red face, your gaze narrows, you have a furrow between your eyebrows, you bite your teeth together and breathe faster."

My jaw dropped down and I realized that I don't deserve the title "Master in hiding anger".

She added, "You know, if you let us know soon enough when you are angry, maybe we can help you before you explode."

Whow! I realized: There is no point in hiding anger, because they feel it anyway. One more little piece of the puzzle that encourages and confirms me on my way from empathy to authenticity. Thank you, girls.

Two years later we rebuilt. The kitchen is now in the biggest room of our house. It is open with a kitchen island in the center where many people can gather around. And whenever I stir the pot now, people can sit opposite to me and keep me company.

117

The laundry basket

This story is around the same time as the previous one. The laundry basket is in the hallway, right in front of the children's rooms. It contains the laundry, washed, folded with care and sorted per child. It is waiting there, to be tucked away in the right closets, by my daughters. It has been standing there for over two days now, and with every additional hour the grumbling in my stomach grows. This time I do take the time for a self-empathy process. I am worth it. I use my laminated cards and stand on the observation. "Laundry is in the basket outside your doors." I take a step forward, onto the feeling. "I'm angry because ...". I step on the next card: The need. "I need respect. And appreciation. And acknowledgement."

Now I leap to the Jackal-Show card. This is the card where you can ventilate all your interpretations, judgements, accusations and criticisms by screaming and shouting. This can provide us valuable information. Usually the need appears here, in a negative, cloaked form, like, "You're so disrespectful!" Now I only have to look for the opposite and I receive the need on a silver platter. For this example, "I need respect." When I got acquainted to NVC, this approach was an extremely helpful strategy for finding my need. I remember one situation where my jackal screamed, "You are such an asshole!" Well hmmm, what's the opposite of "asshole"? That one was a real challenge. It took me two days to figure it out. It was, "I want to see you in all your beauty." That translation was a real eye-opener for me.

But now back to my actual story. I'm standing on the Jackal-Show card:

"Does anybody actually have any idea how much work this includes, huh? Hauling the dirty laundry down to the basement. As always, the basket is overcharged and while carrying it downstairs, clothes keep falling off. So, turning around on the narrow stairs, picking it up preventing anything else falling off, turning again and keeping my balance in the process on the narrow-curved staircase. Arrived by the washing machine in the basement, sorting the laundry by color. Deciding whether to sort dark green with the color wash or is it rather for the dark wash. Damn, too much colored wash for one machine. Hm, I'm sure the jeans can handle dark. Then wash the first load.

After an hour back to the basement to find out: The cycle needs another four minutes to finish. Pfff! Too long to stand here and watch the machine. Too short to go up. If I go up now, I'm sure I'll start doing something else, and then I'll forget about the laundry again and everything will be delayed for at least half an hour. I chose to stay and wait it out. I am under the impression the washing machine and I have a different understanding of the concept of time. The four minutes seem to last for ages. Now, ah, just one more minute. The drum spins. Pause. Again, and again and again and again and I

119

wonder why anyone would build such a thing. If the machine needs ten more minutes, then let it just show those ten f***ing minutes. Now finally it beeps. Three times in quick succession. I leap to the door and pull hard. It's stubborn and remains shut. Instead of opening, all the lights of the washing machine are flashing now. Oh, no, please, no! I take a deep breath and there it comes: A long beep followed by a quiet "click". I try again, this time more timidly and: It opens! Okay, that's it.

I bend down and lift the laundry into the laundry basket. Put the laundry basket on the washing machine - great idea of Frank to put a wooden board over the machine and dryer. Here I have a nice work surface. Next is the sorting: What can be put in the dryer, what wants to be hanged out to dry. Dryer on. Put the next load into the washing machine and hang out the rest of the laundry. Done – at least for the moment. This time I am smarter and set my alarm clock to one hour twenty. The drying cycle should be finished by then.

One hour and twenty minutes later everything runs like clockwork. The washing machine is ready, and I repeat the procedure. Then there is only the folding left - everything to the same size, so the clothes can be stacked neatly on top of each other. And finally, sort the laundry by child 1, child 2, husband and me. I do that in a way that makes it easy to put everything into the closets upstairs. That requires skill! I manage this really well and I am a little proud right now.

Now just carry the laundry upstairs, put mine and Frank's laundry into the closet, (why am I putting Frank's laundry away?), and the children's laundry in front of their doors. The rest is their job. I did all that, I do all that once a week. So, yes, is it too much to ask them to put their carefully pre-sorted clothes in their own wardrobe?

I'm going back to the need card. I want to be seen for everything I do. I want to be appreciated for all that. I'm getting calmer. Then a question comes up, "Do I count? Do I matter?"

I don't really know which card to step on, because it's a realization. I'm shocked. I didn't expect that. I measure the degree of my importance by whether the girls put their laundry in their closets? How stupid is that? It really doesn't make sense! I am constantly being presented with expressions of love, hugs, cuddles, painted pictures, little notes with loving words, and I measure the degree of my importance by this stupid laundry? No wonder it was mumbling in my stomach earlier.

I'm going to make another ground anchor card. One for insights. A light bulb might be a good symbol for the card.

And the laundry thing? It disappeared into thin air. From that day on I put the laundry on their beds instead of in front of their doors. And the basket back to where it belongs. One night at the dinner table I shared how annoying washing the laundry can be for me sometimes. I told it in a funny way and we laughed a lot. From then on, I heard from time to time, "Thanks, Mom, for the laundry."

"Going for a swim" always worked

It is summer and warm. Warm enough to go for a swim. I can barely endure these temperatures indoors. I just want to get out preferably to a lake. When I'm over there I have no "to dos". I can just relish the time with the children and myself. Any given opportunity, I'm off to the lake with our children. I prepare lots of food so we wouldn't starve, and off we go. As far back as I can remember this is how we did it. And everybody knew it: When the sun is shining and mom comes home, she packs food, sometimes a little frenetic, and then we go off to the lake. It was always a pleasant time, everybody was relaxed and had fun.

My younger daughter is 13 now and spends more time in her room. The door is closed. Damn often, too often, according to my feeling. Today I come home from work and she is in the kitchen. I ask if she wants to join me going to the lake. She says "Yes".

During the drive she remains silent. As usual, I ask, "How was your day?"

She says, "Okay."

End of story! When we arrive at the lake, she steps out of the car and immediately starts walking. She walks four steps ahead of me. I only see her back. I'm trotting along feeling stupid. My stomach is rumbling and somehow it hurts.

She spreads her towel and sits in front of me. Again, I can only see her back. My thoughts,

122

"Damn. There's something wrong with her. Did I do something? Maybe something happened at school with her friends or a teacher or maybe it's about a boy? I'd love to know what's going on."

So, I say, "Is something bothering you?"

"No-ow," she says in that certain tone, which sounds annoyed.

I say, "Are you annoyed?"

"No, I'm just tired. I'm going to take a nap."

She lies down on her belly and falls asleep.

I long for contact, or at least clarity about what is going on in her. I sense a huge distance between us, even though she is lying close to me. I am frustrated and helpless. And I want to help. Yes, I really want to do something to make her life more beautiful. It is so obvious that she is unhappy that something is not working out for her. And I want to change that. I want to support her. The best strategy that comes into my mind is: Giving her empathy. But when I ask her, she shuts down even further. I'm stuck, spinning in circles.

She wakes up, lies next to me for a short time and then says, "I'm bored. Can we leave?"

Yes, we can, and we do. My fun factor is minus 20, and I'm relieved when she disappears back into her room at home. Thank God my husband is at home to listen to me. It's good to be able to discuss this. I hear he feels the same way. That helps a little bit. At least I'm not alone.

But then he asks, "Have you ever told her how you feel?"

No. No, I haven't told her. Why not? Because she has a lot to handle anyway. I don't want to burden her with all my crap, too. I also don't want to be vulnerable. And I certainly don't want my feelings to depend on her condition. After all, it's my job to take care of my own feelings, right? And I definitely don't want her to be happy, just to please me. Maybe I'm just not brave enough. Maybe I don't trust enough that I am important and that it is absolutely ok to want something from her. Phew. Confusion. So many thoughts. The questions "What is ok to do and what is not?" and "Who is responsible for what?" spin around in my head. I can't come up with a convincing answer and ultimately, I give up. It's just puberty. Eyes closed and sit it out.

Later that day she comes back into the kitchen and takes a seat in front of me at the kitchen island. I look at her. Suddenly my courage appears, and I say something like, "You know, it tears my heart apart that I can't get in touch with you right now." She lifts her head, looks up at me, looks straight into my eyes. And there it is, the contact I've been longing for. It is so intense that we both have tears in our eyes, and she says, "I don't understand this at all. All this time, you were always here in the afternoon, and all of a sudden you're always gone."

Yeah, that's right. Lately I have been working a little bit longer and I started to meet friends. And was not at home in the afternoons. Yes, it's true. That has changed. I realize that it has changed for good reasons, which I now am ready to share with her. I got so bored sitting around all afternoon waiting for someone to leave their room and "need" me. I felt useless. That is why I started to look for new things to do.

She agrees she no longer "needs" me, at least not as she used to. She is also happy for me, that I found new meaningful things to do in my life. It even relieves her, because she has plenty to handle herself and does not want to be responsible for me as well.

This is the start of a marvelous conversation. We both realize that the old strategies for spending precious quality time together, no longer do the trick. We mourn this together and finally start looking for new strategies. Because now it is no longer about "needing", but about "participating in the life of the other", and about experiencing beautiful things together.

Ever since, we scrutinize the things we want to do in advance. Whether they answer the question: Is what we have in mind suitable for having a good time together? A good time in the sense of "We experience something together and have fun while doing it." This can happen anywhere. So, what we do hardly matters anymore. Then it is only a matter of excluding things that are out of bounds for one of us. With this attitude we all find it much easier to plan family events.

My insight:

To get contact, it can be helpful to show the other person my world. Yes, it takes courage and confidence that I am important enough. Hiding behind empathy is a safe place, but sometimes it is just not enough. And finally, there's the role model function. Children learn what is exemplified to them, not necessarily what we preach or try to persuade them to do. So, if I am brave enough and really show myself with my world, they can observe and test it for themselves: Does that work for me? Isn't what my friends do more helpful? After all, that is what happens at puberty. The adolescents search for their own identity. So, it can be a gift for them to experience how parents master the challenge of finding a balance between "You are important to me" and "I am important to me". This is what my head is saying now - the implementation remains a challenge.

The Nikon

This story just happened. As a writer, this is new territory for me. Up until now, I've always wrote about things I experienced earlier. I'm so excited, I don't really know where to start. Well, Christmas has just ended. Frank bought himself a new camera. A Nikon SLR camera. He tested it during the holidays and is now carefully repacking everything so he can return it. I'm busy writing when Frank enters and sits down at my desk. He says, "I need your opinion on how to proceed with the camera." I look at him, look a little longer, a little closer, right in his eyes. I read in his eyes that he is serious about the question. He also looks somehow depressed. I get curious and close my laptop. "You look disappointed? What is it wrong with the camera?". He sighs, "Yeah, well, it doesn't really work. It doesn't release fast enough for a Nikon."

I let the words sink in. A Nikon. Memories emerge. Frank and I met in a photography class. Adult education center - nude photography. I had a Minolta - everything state-of-the-art with autofocus lenses and all kinds of technical gadgets. He had a good old Nikon. One where all settings are done manually. I can picture him in this way now, in the photo course with his Nikon. His hand always on the lens focusing. He had something "bold" that I fell in love with even then. My heart warms up and a stupid grin appears on my face. I think I'm falling in love with him again right now and I'm recalling memories. We shared the passion for photography. This sense of aesthetics and a curiosity to see things from a different angle. He with his Nikon and me with my Minolta. Back then we went out, fully packed with our camera bags, various lenses, light foils and we took great photos, mostly black and white. We installed a darkroom in the basement where we enlarged the pictures ourselves. This common hobby - it forged us together, we could let our creativity run wild while having tons of fun. It was a great time. Melancholy arises in me. What happened to that?

Of course! We had kids and, in the beginning, we took great pictures of them. Then there were digital cameras, small, handy and practical to take along. With those we went from 'great pictures' to 'nice snaps'. And finally, mobile phones took over, with which we now mostly make selfies. It feels like there are millions of images that need sorting out for the annual photo album. At most you browse it one more time before it ends up on the shelf with the rest of them. What happened? I wonder if Frank feels the same way and I ask, "What would you like to do with the camera?"

"Real pictures. I want to make real pictures. When I have such a good camera body with my hand at the lens, I feel the desire to take real photos again. It's worlds apart to take pictures from a camera or a phone."

"You mean like back then?" I feel something awakening in me, this longing for all the things we had back then, and I say, "I can picture you now, just as when I met you with your honest, robust Nikon with fixed focal length and 'making all the settings manually'. Is that what you mean?"

"Yes, exactly," he says. His eyes radiate with expectation. I suddenly realize that these times are gone. I don't think film rolls still exist. And even if they do, they would cost a fortune. No, this time will not return. No digital Nikon in the world can bring it back. I feel a little sting in the heart area, and I say, "I just realized that it won't come back and it hurts a little bit right now. It's over. Those times just won't return anymore, even with a camera with 'Nikon' on it. Do you feel the same way?"

"Yes, I do."

Now here it is, that unifying moment that precious time together. Together, we mourn that some things are over and won't come back. It's just over and it feels so sad.

After a while he says, "I like to own a camera again, which I can discover totally by myself, which I can explore completely, where I can immerse myself in learning. I enjoy that. I also like to allow myself to take plentiful time to really inform myself. To take time to think about what I actually want to do with it. I have so many ideas. Yes, I want to be able to let my creativity run wild again. I'll return the camera tomorrow and buy myself some photo magazines to thoroughly inform myself and also to get inspired."

I (Gundi) am glad that I closed my laptop earlier and made some time for this. We just had quality time, moving moments. Frank obtained more clarity. I have material for a current story and on top of that we saved a lot of money.

This is how the original story ended. Now it is march. There's something wrong with the previous story. Frank bought the photo magazines and actually spent two days studying them. Now they're in the living room gathering dust on the windowsill. Something is missing. Is that really all there was to it? Where we just supposed to accept certain times were over? I ask myself, what was it that made it better back then?

Then I spot it: Being together. Exploring, discovering, learning, having fun, being proud and doing all those things together. Yes, that's what I'm longing for. We overlooked that part, we missed my part. Again. Now I can pinpoint what's wrong with the story: It's the end. It wants to be lived and re-written again. I long for the togetherness that we had back then. This shared enthusiasm for something, diving into a new dimension, learning together, exploring and discovering the world - together. Mourning together that an old strategy no longer works because it simply cannot be restored is one thing. It brings sweet connection. But looking for ways to meet the needs behind it is the next step. That feels powerful. I call Frank and tell him about my discovery. He gets excited, too. He is in another city at a seminar. We decide that this topic is too precious to be handled on the phone and search a suitable time. Easter Monday is free. Then we will sit down together and once again explore all the needs that we both long for in "an honest Nikon", and then find new strategies. I look forward to it.

My special journey of discovery

I'm mucking out. I open a drawer and discover a transparent cover with notes. On a sheet of paper is the name of a school and a year. I vaguely start to remember it was quite some time ago. We gave a two-day introductory seminar over there. We invited parents, teachers and students. On the first day only a few students where present, about five. The second day, four times as many students showed up. Wow - what a success! Apparently, there was something precious in what we shared on the first day. So precious, that they informed their friends and convinced them to come. Seeing so many young people participating, we immediately changed our program and chose to do a Fishbowl. It works like this: First the young people sit in an inner circle facing each other. The parents sit around them in the outer circle and formulate questions on pieces of paper. The notes get folded and put in the middle of the students. The young people in the inner circle pick a question and discuss their answers in the round. The parents get to hear their point of view from a whole group and not only from their own child. And since there are so many of them in the group, it has a much higher potential. The wisdom of an entire generation becomes visible.

When all the questions are answered the groups switch. The parents go in the inner circle and the children formulate their questions.

I have also experienced this exercise by doing circles with men and women, with mothers and daughters. Amazing! Great exercise!

Holding all these notes in my hands I remember that I had a huge insight in that school. My daughters were of a comparable age as the pupils in the inner circle. One student said, "I just want my mother to realize, she is not the only reason in my life why I feel bad." That relieved me a lot back then, because I actually often thought about whether I could be the reason for my daughter's bad mood.

I also remember that there was a special quality in this coming together. So much honesty and with the honesty came vulnerability. Somehow holy energy.

I sorted out the questions and spread them out on the table in front of me. Again, magic emerged. Every question I read touches me in a special way and I wonder why. Maybe because I see longings in them, mostly for real understanding the other generation. Longing for honesty. Many questions begin with: How do you feel when ...? There is also "care" in there for me, and in the end, I feel so much love in them and in me.

The questions also stimulate me, inspire me. If my child asked me this question, what exactly would it mean and what would I answer if I were really honest with myself. Reading the questions of the parents I start asking myself: Would I also like to know that from my daughters or what exactly would be my question?

And this is exactly what I want to invite you as a reader to do now. Let the questions on the following pages wash over you. Let them inspire you.

My tip: Take your time - it's worth it.

Questions of the children

What's going on in my kid, when he or she asks that question? What does he or she really wants to know? If I was utterly honest with myself - what would my answer be?

- How do you feel when we ignore you or run screaming into our room or slam doors?
- Why do I sometimes have to iron or do the washing up?
- When do you feel hurt by your children?
- Why are you so embarrassing sometimes?
- What are you embarrassed about?
- Why does everything always have to be so tidy?
- Why do I have to clean the kitchen sometimes?
- Why can't you just leave me alone?
- How do you feel when we want to watch a film for example, and you say no and we just don't want to accept it?

Questions of the parents

Do I want to know that about my kid? What is alive in me when I ask that question? What do I really want to know? What would my child answer?

- How do you feel when I say: Why can't you finally do that yourself? Why do I still have to take care of it?
- How do you feel when we are helpless?
- How do you feel when we parents are in a bad mood?
- How do you feel when you always say, "I'll do it right away?"
- Why do you complain when you are given a household task?
- Why do you say, "I don't know" so often? How should we respond to this?
- What is it like for you when we parents argue?
- When do you need support and when do you need your rest?
- Do we ask you too many questions? Do you wish to be left alone more? Do you want more clear announcements?
- What do you find so interesting about the new media?
- How do you feel when you lie to us?
- Do you notice when we are sad and disappointed because of you?
- How do you feel when we yell at you?

My questions to my child

What I've always wanted to know... In a next step perhaps also: What would my child answer?

Here are my experiences with the questions. Sometimes it was enough to put me in the role of the questioner and sometimes answers came.

Questions of the children

Why do I have to clean the kitchen sometimes?
In my hand I hold the piece of paper with this question. Reading the handwriting makes it even more special. It brings me closer to the person who wrote it and a scenario emerges in front of my mind's eye. I'm 14 now. My parents are pretty cool compared to others. We also talk to each other often, so everything is chill. Only sometimes, mom gets kind of weird. When this happens, she gets red spots on the back of her neck and insists that I clean up the kitchen immediately. Then we bicker because I want to disappear, and she insists that I clean up the kitchen right now. Well, I could clean the kitchen - that's not the issue. It's just that I'd like to know what's going on with mom, that's all. In reality, she's actually completely relaxed. I'd also like to know what could help her and whether I can support her.

When do you feel hurt?

The next piece of paper. Wow, what a question! I'm 15, a girl again. I'm looking for my place in life. How do I want to be? I'm experimenting. At home, I'm pretty sure I can trust whatever I do, I'll always be welcome. Or perhaps I'm not. Do I ever cross the line? Is my safe haven in peril? I don't want to hurt anyone, least of all you, because I care about you so much. So please let me know if I went too far. And please let me keep attempting what I want to try. I need this friction in order to grow. I need you as sparring partners to train me in becoming strong. But let me know when I am near your limit, so I don't violate it and risk hurting you.

Why are you so embarrassing sometimes?

The question is on the same slip of paper. So, I'm the same 15-year-old girl. When I say embarrassing, I mean, why do you do things that are out of line? All those things I'm not quite sure others consider cool are threatening to me at first. If the others think it's uncool, I get expelled from the group, and then it's super exhausting to work my way back into the clique. And there's something else: If you do things that my friends think are uncool, then I'm in a dilemma. Then I am supposed to defend you and risk being uncool to my friends myself. And if I want to be on the safe side, then I have to agree you being uncool, too, and that feels like betrayal - terrible! Are you aware of this? Do you know what

139

this means to me? I want you to know how critical this is for me, and I want you to consider this, whenever you do embarrass things. I want you to do them only when you have a damn good reason for it. Are there any damn good reasons? If there are, I'd like to know them. And if not, just for my sake, please don't do it, because it'll make my life so much easier.

What are you embarrassed about?

Same note, same 15-year-old. When I ask that question, I'd like to know if you feel the same way. Do you know what it's like? Feeling insecure? Being a little afraid of what you do is good or bad? Are you also sometimes afraid of being disliked or excluded? Maybe also: Have you ever been in my position? And maybe even further: Are you still there? And then - I probably wouldn't want to admit this, but: How did you deal with it? Is there a way out? And if it's not a big issue for you anymore: How did you manage to make it that way? Will it perhaps just go away? And if it's still an issue, how do you manage it now? Maybe there is also a wish for equality: I admit my weakness, you tell me yours!

How do you feel when we ignore you or run screaming into our room or slam the doors?

Next piece of paper. I'm another 15-year-old girl. I can't deal with my parents right now. We bicker a lot. There's always something wrong with me. They're always picking on me and giving me some bullshit chores. And all these sermons, "If you don't study enough for school..." I am fed up hearing that. I choose to ignore it. Sometimes that works. I just pretend they're air. When it works it´s like being in a safe bubble. Like in the middle of a big, transparent water ball, and everyone who annoys me or wants something from me bounces back. It's a funny picture. Everyone goes "boing, boing". Nobody gets through. This is actually a great solution. It avoids me getting so upset that I have to scream. Screaming at you is really horrible. Slamming the door is slightly better. It's just the door. It´s not like I am offending you. It´s just my anger at the shitty door. And this door can stand it. Believe me, I've tried it many times. And in order for it to bang, I have to swing it really hard. While doing that, I can release a bit of the energy raging inside me. That's much better than screaming at you. I will do that later in my room, more silently and in private, so I don't expose myself. I can't think of anything better, so that's what I do. And yet: I can't stand it, when anyone ignores me. Thinking of being ignored, phew, that's sounds terrifying. And now I think I would like to know, which of these things I do, are equally bad for you, as being ignored would be for me. And perhaps if it were just a little bad for you, I would feel so relieved. I mean, you could blame it on puberty. It's quite normal, right?

As a mother in this setting, what would I answer if I were really honest?

For me, slamming the door sucks. Of course, it does. What else could it be? I'm worried, I have hardly confidence. Of course, I don't. Where should it come from? There's barely any contact. I know nothing about you. And my influence on you is almost zero. I'm desperate and feel helpless. Sometimes I'm scared too. The future I picture in front of me, is looking dark. I am aware that this is only my horrible vision, but it's hard to get rid of it right now. When we meet, you seem so cold - at least to me you do. You're almost permanent in a bad mood. Do you ever feel slightly good? Do you ever enjoy life? You hardly ever show it to me anymore. I want to believe so badly that you are ok, because then I am at ease and can let go. I keep trying to connect but seldom succeed. It is so immense frustrating. And this constant bickering is so exhausting. This walking on eggshells around every word or the wrong emphasis. It drains my energy, it's so exhausting. The screaming is the worst part for me. When you finally flee into your room and slam the door, it's kind of liberating because the screaming stops. Ignoring is okay for me. I can handle that. I tell myself, you're on your period. What I really long for is trust, confidence, letting go and being free from responsibility. Freedom - yes, that feels good.

What can I do to get what I really need?

To feel free, I could take more care of myself. Do things that I enjoy and nurture me. Take some me-time. Find hobbies, maintain my contacts so they blossom again. Do things that give my self-confidence and self-esteem a boost.

To gain confidence in you, I could write down all the things you do well, all the qualities you have, all the things I really appreciate about you and all the things I think can help you in life. I could also paint a nice picture and hang it up in a central place where it would remind me of your strengths. I could also change my horror scenario into a brighter vision of the future. Maybe this is a bit too much being on cloud nine. But I could think of a way to escape my horror scenario show, when it starts. After all, it's only my film.

What could you do for it? You could tell me about things that offer you pleasure. You could tell me who's there for you when you're feeling down. You could gently point out to me, if anything I do comes across as nagging. You could also give me a leap of faith in assuming that I have a good intention in everything I do. And I could do the same for you. Oh, and before we both surrender to our scenarios and let them drag us down, we could both ask the other about her intention.

Questions of the parents

I thought for a long time about what to do with the questions of the adults. Several times I picked up the little pieces of paper. Some of the questions appealed more to me so I wondered why? Then suddenly I realized it: They were my own questions and I went on an exploratory tour.

How is it for you when we parents fight?

I remember a situation in our old house. The children's rooms are situated on the first floor. It's well past bedtime, maybe around 9 pm. We put the children to bed and went to the living room. We are arguing. I don't remember what is was about - one of those mediocre arguments. Not very hefty, not very loud, but already with a certain potential for conflict. At some point I went into the hallway where I saw my daughter. She was around 6 years old. She was hiding behind the shoe shelf in her nightgown. It was cold and dark in the hallway and she was standing there. Oh, my God. My little girl was standing there in the dark and freezing. My heart jumps up. What was she doing there? Was she there because we were arguing? Was she scared?

What a huge question: Is she scared? Was I scared? Memories appear. Memories of me being a child while my parents argued. It was threatening.

Every time that happened, I was afraid my parents would divorce, and I would have to live in an orphanage. Like in the movie "The little princess." I was afraid I would end up in such an orphanage like Shirley Temple, living in a little room under the roof and washing up towers of dirty plates. That was my biggest fear as a child in those days.

Now as a parent having that question in my heart, I want to know if my daughter has similar horrible fears. If she does, I want to comfort and her. I want her to know that getting into conflicts is a part of life. That it´s a normal thing and it happens to everybody. I also want her to know, that when we as parents get into a conflict, it´s our job to handle it, not hers. We are very aware of that and are willing to take responsibility for our relationship. Whatever our disagreements are, we will sort it out and do everything in our power to prevent a divorce. We also know how to do that. We have tools to learn how to argue without leaving any major injuries. And we will use them. And whenever she is afraid again, I want her to enter the living room and let us know. Because then we'll park our arguing and take care of her, comfort her so she can resume her sleep.

I just finished writing this, when my daughter comes in. I ask her if she still remembers this situation. She smiles and shares that she often stood or sat hidden in between the jackets at the cloakroom. It was warm there and even a bit adventurous. Doing something unallowed gave her a thrill. On one

146

side it was an exciting hideout where she remained undiscovered. On the other side she hoped someone would find her. She also wanted to be with the grown-ups since she is the older sister. Additionally, there was curiosity, and the question, "Are you guys okay if I'm not here?" Back then, she wasn't sure.

When asked if she was afraid when we argued, she said, "When you were bickering, I sometimes wondered whether I should intervene to distract and support you, but I can't remember being afraid. I comforted my little sister, who was afraid." So, I asked her sister how she experienced that situation. She answered, "Yes, I was afraid, not of divorce, but that you guys would not get along anymore again. My big sister comforted and reassured me. Those were our most intimate moments."

Why do you keep saying "I don't know"? How are we supposed to react to that?

I know that expression too well. My daughters frequently used it. Sometimes it even appears several times in the same sentence. It's even sneaked into my own vocabulary, so it would be interesting to know why they use it. I ask my daughter and got the following information.

"I don´t know", can express many things: I do not want to answer the question at this moment. I just don't want to tell you the answer. I do not know the answer. I'm not into conversation now. I want the freedom to decide and I'm not willing to commit myself now. The best reaction for parents is to accept that there is no answer at the moment.

"I don't know", can also mean, "I don't want to deal with this topic right now. I have more pressing matters to deal with." Parents could ask then, "When will I get an answer?" Or, "Will you have this information at some point in order to answer the question?"

An "I don't know" that refers to a problem in need to be solved, is not final. It will be often followed by "... but I will sort it out." In this case parents could offer support.

An "I don't know" can also be just a harmless pause filler like an "uh", like a dash. I'm thinking out loud now. Then you better ignore the significance of the sentence.

After all, it's the same with this expression as with anything else. No matter what I say, in the end it is always the intention behind it that matters and not the words themselves. You can't generalize the meaning of this statement. It makes sense to ask directly what exactly is meant by it, in the current situation.

Somehow, I am not much smarter now than before. I do have information, but it is not so satisfying. So, I attempt a different approach. I am asking myself how do I feel when I ask this question and what exactly do I want to know?

Sometimes that expression has no effect on me. Sometimes I notice that it occurs several times within the same sentence and it occasionally surprises me, but not more than that. Sometimes, I react irritated to this statement and sometimes an "I don't know" even annoys me. This happens when I want to plan something and need commitment to do so. Whether I receive an acceptation, or a rejection is less important, but give me something I can count on. Sometimes I really miss reliability in the next generation. Something I get a commitment, just to be cancelled five minutes beforehand - not towards us parents, but amongst each other. And this leads me to ask the next generation: How do you deal with this independent freedom? With this short-liveness and the fast change in decisions? With the lack of reliability? How do you deal with that?

Do you recognize when we feel sad or disappointed?

That could also be my question. More precisely, my question would be: Can you tell when I'm hurt? So how do I feel when I ask this question. I'm torn. Part of me wants you to know and part of me doesn't. Ah, this is exciting. I think I'm trying to hide these feelings for myself, to tuck them away as soon as possible. They are unpleasant. I don't want to feel them. And I certainly don't want to give you the power to make me feel them. Still, sometimes they're present. And your behavior affects me whether I like it or not. And sometimes you do things that hurt me. I'd like you to know that. But I also don't want to put all the blame on you. Exactly, I want to take responsibility for my part, for what I did. And I would like you to take responsibility for yours. Yeah, if everyone takes responsibility for their own part then we have a clean slate. Then we can see what everyone can do to prevent injuries. Would you be willing to do that? That's my real question. And I already have an answer to it. It's yes.

Two days ago, I experienced it myself as I was writing this actual chapter. I didn't quite know what to do with the questions yet. I realized that they carry great potential. I was sitting at the dinner table with my two daughters and my niece who was visiting us, when I had a brilliant idea: With these three people of the next generation present, I could read the questions to them. They could answer them. I could record their discussion transcribe it get to answers and powerful stories. I asked them three and they agreed.

We spend a lovely afternoon together and, in the evening, when I finally asked them if we could start now, the answer was, "Well, somehow there's no energy left for that now." That hit me. Full frontal. I got up. I just wanted to get out of there. My daughter said, "Is that okay with you, Mom?" "No." I heard myself saying. I left the room. I just fled. I was shaking. I needed to get my bearings straight again. What was going on? I was so upset, hurt and disappointed. I focused my attention on my thoughts. The message my brain received was, "The girls are not willing to do anything for me." Ouch! I also heard my brain saying, "They don't care. I don't matter." And probably quite a few more things that go into that direction. What a horror trip.

I'm so glad, I learned some tools to get out of that spiral. One of them is to put the words, "I'm telling myself…" in front of my thoughts. And that's what I did.

"I'm telling myself that they don't care. I'm telling myself that I don't matter." After doing this, I found myself in another world. Now I heard a voice inside me saying, "What?! No way! This is definitely not true. How can you think that? We just had such a beautiful time together. That cannot be true. Now go and seek with them what they really meant." Hearing this was so much better. What a relief. I calmed down and went back inside. They were still sitting over there. The atmosphere was tense, and I heard, "Please come back, Mama, let's sort this out." I hesitated a little. I was still much more agitated than I'd like to be, to engage in a clarifying conversation. They repeated their invitation and added the word "now". So, I sat down. My daughter started, "I'm sorry, I didn't realize it was so important to you. I didn't get it. It is important to you, right?"

"Yes," I said. "I've been waiting all day for this to happen."

"What exactly is important to you? Did you want to experience the quality of a fishbowl with us again?"

"Not really. I know that our setting would not be suitable to get that level of quality."

"Then maybe these questions are *your* questions, and this is why you wanted to hear *our* answers?"

I scrolled through the questions. "No, not really. Some of them are interesting. They appeal to me, but I didn't write them. No, I think I just wanted it to be easy. I thought I could record your conversation about it, transcribe it and then make a story out of it. That would have been super easy. Because earlier, I couldn't come up with anything real, even though I was thinking about it all the time."

"Maybe you wanted to share your world with us."

"Oh, yeah, there is some truth in that, absolutely. That would include you even more in my big project. But the thing that hit me was that I thought I heard you say you didn't want to support me. Is that what you meant to say?"

Now she says, "No. No, I DO want to support you! I understood that this is important to you. That is why I tried to recruit more people. I asked a few friends if they would come over and join us. But when everyone eventually cancelled, there was just not enough energy left. And I trust the energy. At the same time, your book is super important to me, because I do love the stories and I find them all really precious. For me it is absolutely important that it's going to be good. Now when there was so little energy, I no longer had the confidence that it would be good enough. What do you hear me say?"

"I hear that my book is important to you, so important that you're extra attentive and you follow your intuition."

"Thank you. And I want to support you. I just didn't have the confidence that this strategy would be helpful, because they are not your questions, and we are also slightly older than the target group back then. And you wanted this to be real, right?"

"Yes. I did."

My other daughter says, "You could write down what just happened. That would be real."

Yeah, it would be. Much more real than my original plan. "Isn't that too personal, too intimate?"

"No, it's a success story, and it can be written. After all it would be the truth - the whole truth."

"Is this okay with you all?"

I get a "yes." I'm relieved. A lot of tears have been cried during this process. Now everyone is relieved. All of a sudden, the mood is exuberant. Everyone's hugging.

How was it for the daughters?

Claudia Broadhurst, editor of the German NVC Journal "Empathische Zeit" (Empathic Times) asked me to write something about "NVC inside the family". She added, "Because Frank and you are something like 'The Popes of Education'." I had to grin. Oh, are we?

Well, my truth is: I tried to maintain real contact with the children and with Frank, and I think I succeeded mainly. Especially when we used NVC. It was important to me to take them seriously, to really listen to them, to put myself in their shoes. That's why our mutual book bears the title: 'I want to understand what you really need'. At some point it came to me that taking myself seriously is equally important to taking the rest of the family serious. When the tempers overheated, we sat down and together we explored how we felt, what was important to us and how we could make it better for all of us. Sometimes it took me a while to find the courage and strength to do so. Above all it was important to me, experiencing those precious quality moments with each other and just enjoying life. In a nutshell, that's the beauty for me, from my standpoint. I pondered it might be even more exciting, for you as the reader, to find out what it is like, from a child's point of view, to grow up in a family where parents attempt to use NVC. So, I asked them and here are the interviews with my daughters:

Interview with Elia (16):

Gundi: *How was it for you to grow up in an NVC-family? What was different or special?*

Elia: I think you tried to treat us as equals. Not like we have same age, but as equally important and with similar significance as yourselves. I appreciated that very much.

In general, the way you talked to us was different. When we said something, you went into it more deeply, showed more of an interest. Although it was probably not always the most rational thing we said or what made the most sense. You simply responded to our deeper needs. Many years ago, on my birthday I was afraid of a friend in kindergarten. I didn't want to see her on my birthday, because that day was so special and sacred to me. On top of that, I just received a Barbie castle, and it was the greatest Barbie castle in the world. I really didn't want to go. And you guys understood and let me stay home for the day instead of going to kindergarten. So, I could enjoy this special day to the fullest. All day long I played with my new Barbie castle and did not have to encounter the friend I was afraid of. I still remember this like it was yesterday. I am convinced you allowed this, because you understood what it really was about for me. I think I had to be about four years old and up on today I still can recall it vividly. It was so valuable to me.

I also remember the times when I was really happy as a child. Then you gave me that "happy empathy". You said something like, "It makes me so glad to see you happy now!" That enlarged my joy even more and strengthened my feelings.

Another point is, that our bickering was different. I don´t remember feeling hopeless. When I was at my friend's house and she was in a fight, I often cried and was totally desperate. Over there it always seemed as if she could never get along with her parents anymore or understand each other in any way. However, in our family, whenever we had a fight it never got out of control. For me it was always very structured: Everybody got to speak. For every single family member, we explored together, what was important for us and how we felt. And yes, it sometimes was intense and painful to really taste the feelings. Although afterwards I always felt better. With you I never experienced such an escalation where you would run away in anger, leaving me behind all alone. I never saw that in our family.

Gundi: *Sounds like you had the confidence that such a quarrel can also end well?*

Elia: Yes, and I saw the upside from having a quarrel: It can be useful because things get better afterwards. When we argue today, we still use the same structure. We have a script how to handle it. With this structure, disputes are contained, controlled and predictable. (Note from Gundi: see 'Family Conference' from Thomas Gordon. More to that topic in Marie's interview.)

Today we are having profound conversations. We exchange our opinions from different points of view. I find it very pleasant to experience that space for sharing my insights by knowing I will not be condemned and that I never get turned down.

Gundi: *What did you learn from our NVC approach? What impact did it have on you?*

Elia: We had these cards with happy, sad, angry, disgusted and so on. I learned very early the feelings I felt when I liked something or disliked other things. I'm pretty clear of what I want from myself and from others. I form an opinion and stick to it. This is often helpful since I can tell the other what is going on inside of me and I can also choose to do something or not to. Unfortunately, I experienced that some people can't cope with that so well.

I can also show myself as I really am – whenever I want to - and I am also open for people of all ages.

Gundi: *How did that work with your friends?*

Elia: I actually like talking about my feelings, using the four steps of NVC and I like giving empathy. It is sad my normal friends are unfamiliar with that. I can't exactly go and teach them how empathy works or ask them to be more honest. Sometimes I have the impression that they don't understand me at all, and that's sad and sometimes a little lonely.

On the other hand, what makes me happy is that many of my friends come to me when they have problems. I enjoy being the person who actually listens and supports them with what's going on. Besides me I don't think they get that anywhere else. In my opinion, everyone needs someone to listen. I think it's great to take on this role because it makes the connection stronger. Too bad, that it is not totally reciprocal. My friends do their best, but it's not easy for them - they haven't mastered it yet.

I made some friends at an NVC family camp who are familiar to NVC. With them the relationship is much better, much easier, much more honest, much more open and supportive. There it is quite natural that we try to understand our counterpart, to put ourselves in the other person's shoes, to be really emphatic and to listen.

Gundi: *What was unpleasant for you? Where do you see pitfalls?*

Elia: When I had disputes with my friends and I told you about it, I sometimes felt left alone. You also wanted to understand the other children and pointed that out to me. At that time, I would have liked more support. Parents should stand by their own children first. They should protect them and take care of them first. Their own child should be the most important thing. I know today, that you tried to solve the conflicts, which was really difficult and important, too. What struck me was that I thought that the other children were just as important as I was. So, I would have liked you to stand by me. Now I think it wasn't so bad, because I also learned to respect the others.

One more thing I remember is, that we had this family planner. It said who is in charge for what tasks. Everyone had to do stupid chores. I had to bring in the bikes. In my memory it feels like a huge "always". I ALWAYS had to bring in the bikes. I think I did that only once, but it felt like a huge workload. I was five. We had these hated Sunday conversations, where we committed ourselves to do something. At some point the arrangements were forgotten anyway, but when they were fresh, we always had to do them. I didn't like that.

What I also didn't like was, when I got annoyed with some teacher or something alike, and you tried to empathize with me in an extremely calm way. You said something like "Yes. And how do you feel now?" I would have much rather heard, "Oh, yeah, he's really dumb." When I get angry, I want confirmation first. Maybe not always, but most of the time I do. Those empathy attempts brought distance between us. It felt like you were not taking me seriously. It didn't feel natural or real. To entrust my feelings to you, I need to be confident that the interest in me comes straight from the heart. It's really hard when you're angry and someone approaches you with a squeaky voice and with an attitude of: Everything is okay and let's talk in the four steps.

Gundi: *Did you miss any experiences with us using NVC?*

Elia: As a child I really wanted to have house arrest like my friend. I thought if you were grounded, you didn't have to go to school. Room arrest was even better. You were served breakfast in bed, bring it on! Thinking of it now, I am glad I did not get it.

I think I made all experiences. Meanwhile I even had someone yelling at me really loud. It shocked me and made me cry. I have also felt left alone sometimes. Maybe not as often as other kids, but I think I have already felt everything there is to feel. You can't always use NVC either. Sometimes I am too upset and then it just doesn't work.

Gundi: *What would you recommend to people who are just starting using NVC with their kids?*

Elia: What they can improve? In any case it helps to try to empathize with children. For example, when the child doesn't want to go to bed. If I didn't want to go to bed, it was because I was afraid to be alone, or because I just didn't want to be alone. You stayed with me then, and that was nice. It's really bad as a child to be sent to bed with a feeling that your parents are mad at you.

I also think it's important to let children know that there are all sorts of feelings. That feelings are always present, and it is okay to have them. No, even more. They are important! Parents can make it clear to their children that they don't have to hide their anger. They can make clear that being angry is also a natural part of life, and that the parents themselves also feel like this sometimes. I used to think that you couldn't cry. I even thought that you have never cried in your life. If I would have seen that you were vulnerable, too, I would have learned to back off. If I experience only I can cry or get angry, I don't have to care about the others, because they are never worse off than I am.

Gundi: *What about honesty?*

Elia: Whenever a child is screaming and crying and doesn't know what to do anymore it's hard to hear from the parent, "I don't like what you are doing." Even if it is the truth. In this particular moment the child is unable to hear the truth of the parent. It helps more to address it later at a more convenient time. You could then say something like, "Hey, if you do ..., it bothers me, because ... And I would like it to be different. What do you think about that?" Or, "Is it super important to you doing this exactly like you are doing it? Can we think of other ways that don't annoy me?"

I remember your first attempts with NVC. You talked in the four steps straight from the book. That was funny and strange at the same time. I think it's important that you integrate NVC into your life, live and breathe NVC in such a way that it's almost unnoticeable. When you manage to talk in four steps without anyone noticing it, then you're a natural.

Interview with Marie (18):

Gundi: *What was different with NVC?*

Marie: All my friends were complaining, how stupid their parents were. But concerning you, they always said that you are cool. Even now they think we are a dream family, always having fun and enjoying each other. And it's true. Often, we sit around the table and fool around. We laugh a lot, are honest and open with each other and we tell each other a lot, too. I think that's what many other families lack. After all, I always found our parent-child relationship very nice. Loads of connection, tons of exchange and all of that wrapped in a friendly relationship. Never this opposition. Nevertheless, I never wanted to clean up my room. I gladly postponed that. We survived that, too, without damaging our precious relationship. I still don't like cleaning up, but it slowly grows on me. I have to, otherwise I can't move anymore and only stumble around the room.

In the beginning there was the "formal NVC" with sterile feelings and needs it sounded somehow unnatural. Later it became more natural and helped us to maintain real connection. I always perceived you guys being very relaxed, very open minded. For example, when I wanted to go to a party you trusted me to make the right decision.

Which I did in return. I never felt an urge to do anything in protest against you. I never had the need to rebel against you, not in a self-injuring way. I never been binge drinking, because there was nothing to resist to. On the contrary, there was a vast amount of trust and confidence that made me grow independent. If I wanted to be sick at school, I didn't have to lie by saying my stomach hurts. I simply said, "I don't have any important classes today and I'm really tired. I'd like to rest today." Or, "I'm afraid of math." You said, "Think about it." And no matter what I decided, you went along. That's how I learned to make my own decisions and take responsibility for them. If I'm afraid of math and don't go, it'll just make it worse. So, I decided I'd rather start studying and accept support. And I learned to take care of myself. When I'm really exhausted, I allow myself time to recover and that's perfectly okay. That was different with other kids. They had to lie to their parents about everything, and then of course there was distrust on the parents' side. What a pity.

What I also noticed is that my friends did absolutely no effort to understand their parents. You don't always have to give them empathy. But you can at least try to understand them why it's extremely important for your mother to put the cup IN the dishwasher or take your feet off the table. I didn't always understand why certain things where so important to you when you repeated them for the sixth time, or you raised your voice.

But I thought: There seems to be something behind it. So, I can just go along and do what she asks! And the other way around, too. I just know that if something is important to me the principle is: I will be understood, and it will probably be done.

It is all about taking us seriously. You always took us seriously and together we examined what's behind it all. And often there was a lot behind it. Especially during puberty. Of course, that's a phase to go through, and still there is always something precious behind it worth to be explored. I was visiting a friend when her mother came in asking her to remove her feet from the living room table. My friend sneered back, and then they bickered a bit and the mother went, "Oh, puberty!" And my friend's like, "F***ing mother." Gosh! Such a thing would never occur in our family. There would have been a completely different mutual understanding. We would have tried to make life more beautiful for each other. There are many situations that can be made more beautiful with mutual understanding. I've experienced that over and over again and I really like it.

Another topic is self-responsibility. For example, with the school grades. No matter what grades I got. It was always okay for you. You never praised me for an A, and I was never ridiculed or even punished for a bad grade. Everything was always okay. Although the grade itself did something to me. When I got an A, I would come home and celebrate, and you would join me and be with me in my joy. If I was sad because I got an F, it wasn't so bad, because I knew when I came home you would hug me, and I could weep it all out. That was really beautiful. Then we examined the cause: Did I just have a bad day, or did I need support and how could that support look like? Sometimes I learned math with my dad. But I had the final responsibility for my own grades. You also never took anything away from me. It made me independent, and now I'm doing pretty good. I'm in 12th grade, and math is a bit too fast for me. But I want good grades. In my final year of school, it's not just about surviving the year. So, I requested tutoring classes. Very quick you made it happen, no questions asked, no strings attached.

Gundi: *What did you like very much? What were the outstanding highlights?*

Marie: I witnessed your whole process of immersing yourself in NVC. I was five when you started. We grew up with it and we grew closer with it. I remember a big fight that you and I had, when I was four. We stood on the stairs and we were both really pissed off. And then you slapped me, it was horrible. I ran into my room and I kicked the bed. I was in such pain and completely entangled in my helplessness. Probably you felt the same. That's when you started reading books, attended courses and it just kept improving. The more I aged, the less we got into situations where we felt complete helpless. When I look at where we're standing now, it's a giant leap. Really cool!

There were also funny experiments depending on the book you were reading. I had a fight with Elia once, something with Lego. We were pissed at each other when you showed up. You were probably waiting for a suitable moment to try out your new skills. We were asked to sit on the couch, and then you asked, "Like what animal are you feeling right now?"

Elia and I looked at each other in utter confusion and said, "Huh, what is she up to?"

You, "Do you feel as angry as a lion?"

We, "What? How does a lion feel? I have never felt like a lion before."

You, "Just try to roar like a lion. Roar it all out."

We went, "Aaah."

You, "No, do it with more anger!"

We a raised our voices, "Aaaaarrrrgh".

We were completely confused. So, we quickly made up again. At some point you noticed it missed the effect you were hoping for and you left the room shaking your head. You probably made some evaluating notes. Elia and I glanced at each other and said, "What was that all about? Never mind, let's just continue to play."

There were also the hand puppets. The giraffe, the jackal and ears of both. They made it more tangible, I liked them. I remember you and dad were bickering once. Elia was scared and I comforted her. We sat in front of your door and discussed: What shall we do? We fetched the giraffe ears, I quickly ran into your room, put them on the table and ran out again. I think that made a difference.

Gundi: *I remember that too and it actually made a big difference. It moved me a lot. It acted as a wake-up call, reminding me of what really counts and on how we choose to interact with each other. We both pulled ourselves together and sorted out our differences.*

Marie: And then there were those family conferences, which I really liked. Admitted, sometimes they were also a bit annoying, because we had to sit down at the table for ages while the whole nice playing afternoon vaporized. It was obvious in a family of four, there were always frictions that called for attention. Each time something went sideways among us or someone needed more help with housework for instance. We had a list on the fridge and whenever one of us had a topic that needed to be discussed, we wrote it on that list. And on Sundays we gathered around that table. We started by collecting what we wanted to discuss. Second, we wrote it down and finally we processed all of it. It was always the same structure. I liked it because it was predictable and reliable. Everything important we said, was written down and got tangible by that procedure, we could hold on to it. We kept doing that until everything that

169

had to get rid of our hearts, was out on the table. Then we collected suggestions for solutions. It was also always important for us to find a consensus. We have never been satisfied with a compromise. That was sometimes exhausting, but it was worth it. In the end everyone committed to it, by putting their signature under our agreement.

I remember one example that was really important for me. It was about staying up longer than my sister. She was three years younger than me. And I realized, I wanted to be seen in my "being older", and to be taken serious about that topic. After all I was already seven and almost a grown up anyhow. As a result of our family conference I was allowed to stay up longer. I think five minutes or something like that. But the number didn't matter. The main thing was that I was allowed stayed up longer. It turned out to be pretty boring, because I had no one to play with and TV-time was already over. In those spare minutes, you and dad talked about things that didn't interest me at all. But I was allowed to stay up longer, and that mattered, because I was taken seriously. So, I learned from the start: If there are problems, you gather around the table, talk about it until we find a solution that makes it better.

I also remember there was talking stick. When I disagreed with my sister, you did a little mediation with us. It had a special structure. We couldn't do it by ourselves like that. It was nice having a mom, who made sure that everything was said, everyone was heard, so we could find solutions and it would be okay again. As far as I can remember it, it always turned out good.

Gundi: *What was the impact on your female friends?*

Marie: If someone came up to me and wanted to speak ill of her friends or her parents, that was difficult for me. I didn't want to play a part in that. So instead, I tried to empathize, to understand them a little, to give empathy or just simply hear them out. I found that difficult because I didn't have those "normal teenage problems". Middle school was the center of gossip. I couldn't do anything with it. It was terrible for me. The main topics of conversation were about the others: What he or she was wearing. What he or she had done, and I couldn't get into it at all. That always made me a bit of an outsider. Later at parties, they filled themselves with alcohol, and I took on more of a mother role, by looking after them.

I also had difficulties with their way of talking. It was so different. I didn't understand it. Why don't they just say what they mean? Why do they hide? Especially when they talk to their parents. Why do they make their own lives so complicated?

When they fought amongst themselves, I was the safe haven. Everyone came to me wanting to spill it all out. Unfortunately, always in this gossip manner, really hard to understand. It took me a while to deal with it somehow, because I was unfamiliar to it. When we argued at home, we quickly got to the emotional level and then to the needs. But when someone came up to me and said, "She's so stupid," it was really exhausting to be empathetic. And even if a feeling finally appeared, they quickly revolved to their familiar pattern. Maybe because feelings could be dangerous. Real connection with my friends was difficult and I missed it. I had much higher expectations, because I was much closer in contact with the people in my family, than with my friends. That was really a pity. I even wondered what friends are for, if there was so little connection. I guess I never really belonged in their group. I was more like the odd one out. But we were friends anyhow. They appreciated me because I had a special role: When they argued, they came from both sides to me and cried their hearts out. Of course, I wasn't allowed to say anything to the other and therefor I stood between them. Nevertheless, I liked the role. After all, I had a mission, where I didn't had to bend or even betray myself too much. I wanted to belong to the group, but never in a way unfaithful to myself. And that worked out fine. Today I have friends with whom I have a more beautiful, more real connection.

Gundi: *What did you learn from this? What did you get out of it?*

Marie: A profound connection with myself from which I derive strength. I can understand myself and by that, I am able to understand others. I can really empathize with other people. Feeling my own feelings doesn't scare me. Neither does seeing the feelings expressed by others. Normal people are often completely helpless when an adult cries. For me it's an expression of a feeling and it's perfectly okay just like laughter.

I can also see the beauty in being different. NVC has also helped me to find out who I am and what's important to me. I can get in touch with myself, have a good look: If I feel bad about something - what's behind it? Sometimes I have a "growl" with a person and ask myself: Why? NVC shows me the way to get out of that uncomfortable feeling. I can explore it and address it. It's really worth it.

As a child I was reluctant to show my emotions in conflict with my sister. I was afraid it would escalate and make things worse. I thought if I hide my feelings, it would only hurt me, not her. Then I experienced over and over again, that things improve, when I show my true self and when we are able to talk about it, in a controlled and safe setting. Afterwards it's vanished, out of my heart. In most cases it even leads to a stronger connection whereas I originally was afraid of the opposite. These experiences encourage me to speak up, to

173

show my emotions and to trust it is exactly that, what will preserve the relationship. I've also realized it gets worse, when I leave matters unspoken. Unspoken matters tend to grow and pop up everywhere, like a vicious circle.

Sometimes there were very strong emotions when we argued - that was pretty scary. I remember when I was 14, I went to Canada for two months by myself. I attended self-discovery classes. Coming of Age and Vision Quest. I changed tremendously and made enormous progress. Meanwhile you lived your usual lives at home which barely changed. And then when we met again, I had a hard time just looking at you. It was like a storm front that collided. I would have been pissed off by the slightest thing you would do. When a person changes a lot or went to a growth spurt, the relationship has to adapt also. It needs to be rearranged. Just like a snake can't stay in its old skin. I had similar change struggles with my sister. Each time she took an evolution leap, we had to find each other again.

Gundi: *What was not so good? Where do you say, "Hey guys, don't do that!"*

Marie: Which I disliked, in the beginning or further on, was when you so stuck to formalities. Whenever I was experiencing an emotion, right in the middle of expressing my fiery energy, you said,

"Wait a minute, I'll just get the four-step cards." Then you placed them on the floor, and you told me to stand on the emotion card and I was supposed to say, "I feel like this." At that point I thought, "Mom, what are you doing?" This is not real anymore, it is artificial, it took all the fire and life out of my feelings. Feelings simply want to be felt and treated in their own intensity. Not broken down into little cards. Whenever you made me walk these cards, it felt like being constrained in some box. The message I heard from you was: What you experience now is completely normal, now let's follow the pattern - as if I were a pattern! I am anything but a pattern. I was in this situation, it was so real to me, so unique and I definitely did not fit into a pattern. It was a violation against the individuality of the moment. I had the idea that you didn't understand me at all. I felt like an experiment and thought, "Now she's happy that I'm upset, because then she can finally try her stupid four steps." It was like you didn't even want to know how I was doing, and I was just a guinea pig in your laboratory.

But that wasn't the case at all. You were doing this because you cared about me and because you wanted to support me. It's a pity that this message didn't always get through.

On the other hand, this structure did offer support. However, it would have been ideal, if the four steps came unnoticed, in a more natural, more lively way. So that you have the four steps at your disposal, somewhere in your backpack, without clinging on to them so stubborn. Just use their guidance in a more fluid, flexible way, surf along with the flow of the moment. Just observe: What's present at the time? What is needed right now. Then I could skip the need, return to the feeling and then back to the need. Of course, that approach needs a lot of practice. You have to fully comprehend it, before you can let go of the pattern. I also understand that it is a long way to make it sound natural.

It would probably be best, if NVC is applied unconsciously. So, whenever the child gets upset and is totally emotional, you as a listener are aware: It has absolutely nothing to do with what happened and you don't have to do a thing about that. Instead it is all about the child feeling like shit right now. This bad feeling wants to be expressed until everything is out. And when everything is ventilated, the need will appear naturally. Then you can say something like, "Hey, why is that so important to you? Why does it bother you so much when that happens?"

You might get an avoiding response like, "Yeah, I can't because..."

Then you can ask, "What is really important to you? What do you actually want? What do you want him to do?"

Just like that. All natural. It is also not important always to name correct needs and feelings, they can sound strange and sterile. It is extremely irritating to hear, "No, you can't feel that, because that's not a pure feeling." This stops all progress, so don't do it!

What does help instead, are suggestions. I always liked it when you think and feel along with me, because often I couldn't come up with the words. When I was too excited and angry, I just said something like, "That's so f***ed up!"

And then you say, "Are you disappointed maybe? Are you also...?"

That made me continue to talk, you joined in and we finally got to the need naturally. At that point it is helpful to ask, "What would you like the other person to do? What would YOU want or what would help you now?" You can also ask, "If you were to ask him for something now, what would it be?" instead of commanding, "And now your request!"

But I truly understand that it's difficult, especially in the beginning. That's okay, things can't always be easy. Maybe it helps to state your intention and say something like, "Hey, I'm really trying to help you. I realized that I didn't manage to understand you by doing it the old way. That is why I'm trying a new way." You might as well say, "I'm still learning how to do it. I wish I would be better in it already." And, "I care about you! This manner I use, is simply helping me listening to you." The important thing is, whatever you say it should fit you. Find words that suit you instead of ready-

177

made ones by the book. Important is that what you say comes out your heart and tells your truth.

Another piece I don't like is that you were normal parents in the beginning. Then you discovered NVC and wrote the book. (I want to understand what you really need). Along the way you became more and more famous, and now there are those fans of the first hour who almost think you are idols, they hardly dare to talk to you. When we meet these people, we are sometimes almost treated as "holy". That makes me the celebrity child and thus already completely explained. As if my task in life was being an "NVC child". NO! They don't even bother to ask, "Who are you actually? What do you like? What do you do?" And I think to myself: Hey, hello guys! I want to be seen as an individual, not just as the NVC child. It's like a label or a stamp. Yes, that is also me, but I'm more, also something of my own, and my interests don't really point to the NVC direction. It is simply not my thing. I am more interested in environmental protection or other projects and art and sports. And: I'm not better than anyone else, for heaven's sake.

Sometimes I get asked, "How's that for you?" and, "That must be great." Yes, it's helpful and great, and at the same time it creates the pressure of expectation. Then I think they expect everything I say to be perfect NVC, otherwise I'll stab my parents in the back. It's exhausting. I don't want to be seen as a result of that's how it is, when it works.

In reality I am simply human. I also mess around. I occasionally do stupid things and also say things that are not exactly NVC.

Gundi: *What advice would you like to give young parents?*

Marie: Give it a try! We sat on the couch roaring like lions and it didn't work, and we were so confused. So, what? It was okay. The day after you returned with something new. Especially children easily forgive you, so just try and see what works and what is best for you and your children. Simply trial and error. It doesn't necessarily have to be NVC. You can also find something else. NVC worked fine for us.

The thing I find most beautiful is the giving of empathy. To accompany a person when she feels something. Just the quality of you being there, with her, empathically. Especially with children, but actually with everyone. Simply to acknowledge there is something precious behind everything, deep treasures especially in grief and anger. Even when it is difficult - it is worth sticking with it, to take plenty of time and find out what is really happening.

I also think it is important to really allow feelings in yourself. To truly feel them, to take them seriously and to explore them: What are they doing to me? What do they show me? What do they want to tell me? Just taking care of yourself.

Finally, to take the children seriously. I always very much enjoyed that you treated us as if there was a miracle inside of us.

Gundi's resume:

Phew. Actually, I hoped this was going to be quite simple. I thought I would just do some interviews. Instead I ended up in a rollercoaster of emotions: There was celebrating together, relief in many places, gratitude, sometimes pride, being moved, being agitated, and sometimes it hurt like hell. Especially this one situation that I will never forget because it was so terrible for me: When I slapped my daughter. I lost contact with my daughter and also lost contact with my heart. There was a concrete wall blocking the way to my heart preventing access to my love. It still hurts like hell when I think about it. And at the same time, it was the starting signal for me. I set off and stayed on track. Adjusting my course frequently, to remain on that path. I can second what Marie mentioned earlier: It's gigantic where we landed and I'm tremendously grateful that I came across NVC to be a very helpful tool. I'm also proud of myself for using it over and over again, to the best of my ability at that particular moment.

Highlights from my NVC-life

My first great field of exploration was empathy. I could hardly believe it: Just a moment ago my counterpart was still very upset, and all it took was just some space and perhaps some curious empathy attempts. This according to the pattern: Are you perhaps ... (feeling) and do you need ... (need)? This pattern was highly unusual at first, I had to force myself to pronounce the words. But its effect convinced me swiftly otherwise. A couple of times back and forth, and then ... bull's-eye! "Yes, this is exactly what it's all about." Accompanied by a deep sigh. The whole unrest, this agitated life in my counterpart was transformed into tranquility, inner peace and cheerfulness.

I was so fascinated that I tried it out wherever I could and made many wonderful discoveries. I explored whether there were hidden needs in everyday sentences. And when I read stories to the children, I took short breaks and together we pondered about how the 'witch' from Rapunzel, for example, was feeling and what she might need when she caught the neighbor stealing her beloved salad.

Whenever my counterpart reached that point of deep relief, I was fulfilled. I believe that it is above all my needs for effectiveness, contribution and connection that are particularly nourished in this process. And because it nurtured me so much, the credo "empathy first" became my wisdom.

Empathy was also my first tool to approach conflict. I would say I was a 100 percent conflict shy before. I remember a constellation exercise in which I banished the conflict. I locked it out of the door. But now I was able to listen and trying to understand what it was all about for the other person. What a gift. It is not without reason that our first book is called "I want to understand what you really need". I often experienced that understanding my counterpart led to a huge change in my attitude. Understanding what is so precious for my counterpart, brought these 'Herzspitzen-berührung' (Heart-Touchings) along with comforting, warm feelings accompanied by sweet tears of joy. We bathed together in an ocean of connectedness and understanding. The original trigger now had a different effect and the conflict simply vanished.

At the first NVC Family Camp we joined, I met Kirsten Kristensen. Her wisdom was "honesty first". A friend and I were sitting at the table with Kirsten when the friend's son showed up with a "Mommy can I...?" question. Kirsten said to her, "Tell him, tell him your truth."

My friend answered, "But I can't give him an answer right now because I don't have the nerve to decide that right now. I just need a little tranquility time right now."

"That's exactly what you can tell him. This is your truth." Kirsten said.

She did and added a time when they could talk about it, and he left. He wasn't overjoyed, but he accepted it. This scratched at my image of the perfect mother who always has to be there for the children, who should always put herself aside whenever a child needs something. A while later I met Marshall B. Rosenberg at the International Intensive Training (IIT) in Budapest. I attended his seminar, and something he had said there kept me busy. So, I gathered all my courage and went to him during the break and formulated a question. It was about education. He looked at me and said, "Do you have children?" I said, "Yes, two daughters." Then he said, "If you have children and think there's such a thing as a 'good mother', you're in hell." Damn, busted, seen-through. How did he know that so fast? I started thinking about it and discovered a lot of "shoulds" in me. A good mother should ..., a good wife should ..., a good daughter should ... and so on. Every single one of them was accompanied by a tightness in my throat and chest. Like a corset that restrains me from breathing. And I began to transform these beliefs into, "I want to ... because..." or into, "I choose to ... because..." An adventurous journey from the "I must/should" planet to the planet of conscious choice. I had a lot of work with that, but it was so liberating. Sometimes even intoxicating and I could breathe much better.

I received a list of needs from Klaus Karstädt. Every day I allowed myself a time window of ten minutes in which I started to translate and integrate those new 'need words' into my own language. My vocabulary lacked so many of them and they sounded so bulky. I wanted to find words that suited me so my counterpart could understand them - especially the children.

When I finished that, I started to write a diary. Again, ten minutes a day. I wrote down the things I experienced, defined the trigger, explored my feelings and needs, and depending on the situation celebrated or mourned and finally looked for more helpful strategies. That's how we discovered celebrating and gratefulness for ourselves. I remember I wrote on a red post-it addressed to my husband: 'Hello darling, I decided to celebrate again as from today.' Frank laminated it and I just now rediscovered it. I placed it besides the balcony door. It is completely bleached out; the writing is barely legible.

We also implemented it in our daily life as a family. At dinner we had celebration rounds, and I still remember Elia at an NVC family event, she said in the round, "I celebrate that we are celebrating." It brought so much gratitude into our lives and focused our attention on the beautiful things.

There were many more steps of growing. Listing them all would overdo it, especially since they are not so alive in me anymore. At most they can make me smile. Still worth mentioning is my growing with the children which was always characterized by the topic of "letting go in trust".

One more thing I want to celebrate. When I became a trainer, I defined my role as wanting to be empathic, understanding and giving space to everybody else. I tended to do this even if I joined seminars as a participant. Three years ago I was attending a multiple day seminar as a participant, my husband being one of the six trainers. In this setting, as a community, we succeeded in creating a safe space in where empathy was omnipresent. I gladly and often offered my emphatic listening as a gift. It nurtured me in many ways. I felt precious, valuable and important. Besides it is also safer to give empathy than to receive it. To show myself in my weakness, to be vulnerable, to show myself in my inability. That requires a lot of confidence.

And now the time had come. It was my turn. I was together with a participant that I could fully rely on. She was totally centered and balanced. She offered me her presence and I accepted it. After all I was a participant also! She accompanied me in my process. I got in touch with my grief, which pointed to my longing to be "seen". She mentioned how precious she found it, that I really want to be there for others and what a gift I am to the community. Mmh, I liked that. I could easily take that in,

185

and it warmed my soul in a familiar way. But then she said, "I don't actually know anything about you, and I am curious about you. And you know: If you want to be seen, it does make sense to show yourself." At that moment, it struck me like lightning, and I realized that I am scared. Oh my God, so true! How right could she be! If I hide, if I don't show myself, nobody can see me. How could they? Then she added, "Wow, right now, at this moment, I see you. I can see you in all your beauty. All of your humanity." Her eyes are huge, and what I see in them, is unconditional loving acceptance, and that feels soooo good. I experienced: I am allowed to show myself, there is room for me and lots of love. What she said, was so obvious, and I realized that my empathic accompaniment is a very helpful strategy to get in touch. A well-known, proven and also safe strategy, where I stay in my comfort zone. Showing myself, even exposing my vulnerable side, is another option to get in touch. The quality of connection that can be created by it is of another kind, a more profound one. A new flavor perhaps. In addition, a balance of giving and taking is created plus the possibility to feel how precious it is to be 'accepted'. It's the icing on the cake. To show myself requires a lot of courage and trust and at the same time has the potential to 'be seen'. More than that, it is even the prerequisite to 'be perceived'. Wow. What an insight. What a challenging and also exciting path to follow. So, now, when I join a seminar as a participant, and we are divided into small groups to do an exercise on our topic, and somebody asks who wants to start, I hear myself saying "I would like to go first" more and more often. And I like it. It is so much easier since I am not defining myself as a trainer anymore. It's my turn now.

And finally, there are still topics I can grow in. Especially this 'honesty' thing. I am still on the way to gaining confidence, that my share counts, and that I am safe even when I put my part on the table, when it comes to conflict. It is still challenging and scary for me to tell my truth. At the same time, I do trust that life will bring me plenty of opportunities, to overcome this fear. I'm ready for the challenge.

Thank you...

Rudy! I am so grateful that life brought you on my path. I so much enjoy what you are making out of my poor translations. When I get the stories back from you and reread them, I fall in love with them again. They really gain so much quality and at the same time they still sound like my words. What a challenge. You wrote to me "I do my utmost to stay as close to the original German text and to the Gundi as I know her." It worked so well for me. You mastered it. Also, knowing that you are passionate about editing this book makes it so easy for me to receive your support.

And finally, I want to thank you for being in the same boat with me. It´s a "both of us" project. We can celebrate it together. That is so much more fun than doing it alone.

Thanks to my girls in the home group. It was through you that I discovered my passion for writing. I never knew I had it in me. It was a painful journey for all of us, and yet it made this book possible. Especially to Jutta, for the countless telephone calls in which you inspired me and helped me when I got stuck again.

Thanks to Marie - you listened to my stories and had tears of emotion in your eyes every time I finished reading. And then you once said to me, "Mama, you should write your own book. Your stories are so precious. And when I hear one, it takes me a whole day to process it, in order to be ready for the next one." It strengthened the faith in myself.

Thank you, Elia. Among so many other things, you gave me the hint, "Just write!" And so, I did. Whenever an idea like, "I can't do it at all!" appeared, I remembered your words and just kept writing instead of giving in to my doubts. And it worked. I never knew I was capable of something like that.

So, Frank. Now it's your turn. Thank you for the preface. When I read it, I just had to cry. It felt like: Forever. And, there is more: All these years we've been travelling this path together. Together! With ups and downs. For better or for worse. That were our vows. And we have adhered to it. And we made it through it, together. And I thank you for sticking with it, sticking with me. For letting us share this together, our life. From the Gundi with the hot Alfa Romeo Spider and the Frank with the Passat; from the Gundi with the bling-bling Minolta and the Frank with the Nikon, to what we are today. Just a few years older, but we remained the same in our hearts as before – free, unattached and rebellious. I am looking forward to more of that.

Thanks to my mum. I had the chance to go a different way than you, and I thank you for not judging me for it but being proud of me. Thank you, that means a lot to me. I will never forget this moment: I had given you some of my stories to read, and then I came home from work and was eager for your feedback. I remember it so well. I came to you in the kitchen, and you were preparing the food. Then you turned around and said to me with tears in your eyes, "I didn't know what a precious person you are." Thank you for seeing that in me.

I also thank little Iffi, our dog. Whenever I sat down to write, she never left my side. They say that dogs like to be where there is beautiful energy. So, I just choose to believe in that and thank you, little poop for reminding me in what precious energy I am right now.

There is also Sonia, my editor for the German book. I thank you for having seen a book in my stories. Thank you for believing in me. I also discovered a soulmate in you. I appreciate the lightness in our working together and that you were there for me. I could rely on you. Thanks for that. It made it so easy for me. You once said to me on the phone, "Your stories are like a golden ray in life." I wrote it down in my notebook. Every time I was overcome with doubts, I read that sentence. I framed it so I could find it faster. It nurtured me with faith in myself. What a precious gift.

Finally, thanks also to all the people who have put their trust in me and let me accompany them. Only through you it was possible to experience all that I can share here.

About the translation.

I am Rudy, Rudy Begas from Belgium and I poses a strong need to learn and to contribute. That's why I chose the path of communication trainer, since 2004 full time. I train organizations in the UK, The Netherlands, Germany but mainly in Belgium. I get hired for my contagious enthusiasm and my interactive and playful style of training people. It managed to increase people's motivation and commitment. You can find me on LinkedIn or rudy@begas.be.

In this light, the vast majority of books I own, are self-development books. Since they are 'my books' (I bought them with my own money) I can do with them as I please. I tend to underline words or passages in ink, write thoughts, associations and annotations in the margin. As I come to think of it, I don't really read books, I study them. I want to understand the message the author is trying to teach me. Sometimes I reread a book and pride myself on discovering even more wisdom in it, resulting in even more notes. To really get to the heart of the intended meaning, I prefer to read a book in its original language. When I compare the translated book with the original writing, I sometimes get frustrated, even angry. Sometimes I find literally translated words, sometimes the words made perfect sentences, only they often missed the point.

Since 2012 I discovered NVC and that gave my life and work a boost in meaning. NVC really changed my life. The facts and reality are still the same as before, only, NVC changed the way I perceive and handle my observations. It also changed the way I deal with people in general, my trainings and myself. On that NVC path, I encountered Frank and Gundi on an intensive course in France. Now, a couple years later, I am a candidate for International NVC trainer and Frank is my assessor.

For rare added value seekers, I exhibit a supporting library on a little table next to my classroom trainings. It consists of books on the subject that I teach. NVC-books make up the lion's share of my small collection. I have several sets of books, so I can vary depending on topic and training level. And sometimes when I am ashamed of the translations, I recommend the original language.

My particular vision on translations and studying books, generated some pressure to make a translation myself. On top of that, this opportunity of translating, granted to me, was all about vulnerability. First of all, Gundi's vulnerability, because she exposes sometimes private experiences and inmost thoughts. And at the same time, my own vulnerability, because I want to pass on the wisdom and magic concealed in her writing, to honor the true message. I want to make sure my translation really grasps the underlying meaning of her writing. That's why I read the chapters over and over again, until I got the idea that I fully comprehend what little gift Gundi presents to the reader. When I think I got that message clear, I can start sculpting the English text around it.

In every single of Gundi's writings, I was touched by her being touched (hence the title). Those little wonders struck me each time. I recall translating one of her stories in the middle of the night and I felt disappointed. It was missing the magic! I found no stunning insight, no life lesson. How could she post this story? Until it came to my mind a few moments later (some stories ask for some time to sink in) and then the magic hit me twice as hard. I felt guilty judging her that way, at the same time, that was a gentle reminder how to deal with my own judgements.

So, when a story was translated in a first version, I stored it in a separate folder and let it mature for some time. Often adjusting words or phrases until I felt it was worthy of her intentional meaning. That's how I added my own translating vulnerability. (I still struggle with my perfectionism) And only when I was absolutely confident about it, I did send that story to her, ready to be conveyed to the reader. Those adjustments came from even deeper insights and could surface at any time of the day (or night). Just as I am writing this text to you on my vacation right now. Sitting in the corridor of the hotel, way past midnight, high up in the mountains, bubbling with excitement.

As I write this, I feel a lot of gratitude for you, dear reader, for purchasing this book and even reading it thoroughly until the very end. I hope you are as inspired as me by these little precious gems Gundi offers. Like me, I hope you crave even more of those uplifting stories! And maybe, like me, you discovered that Gundi showed you the path, illuminating the next steps for you. So even in the smallest of things of everyday life, you and I can continue in her spirit, making the world an even more beautiful place, and 'write' our very own coffee cup stories.

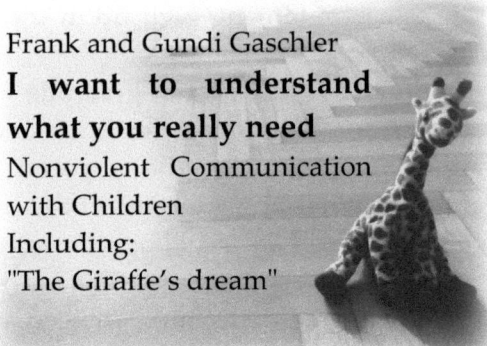

Frank and Gundi Gaschler
**I want to understand
what you really need**
Nonviolent Communication
with Children
Including:
"The Giraffe's dream"

A guide for parents, childcare workers and pedagogic staff. Including "The Giraffe´s dream" – a project of implementing the consciousness and tools of Nonviolent Communication in pre-school institutions.

I went to schools for 21 years and I can't remember that anyone asked me how I felt or what I needed. Instead I was taught things like "right" and "wrong", "good" and "bad" to fit in a system that measures people by these standards.

I recommend the project "The Giraffe's dream" to educators, teachers, parents and children as one way to help each other to do the one thing, we all love to do most:

To enrich people's lives!

Marshall B. Rosenberg